EARLY KINGDOMS
OF THE
GREAT ZAMBEZI:
A BRIEF HISTORY

Imprint by ©thamesbooks
UK and South Africa
©Mayeta Mpondza, 2021
902
The moral right of the author has been asserted.
UK Copyright, Designs and Patents Act 1988.
Cover designed and typeset by thamesbooks in London.
Printed in London, UK.
First published: 2021
ISBN: 978-1-7399374-9-2
All rights reserved. No part of this publication may be reproduced, stored in a retrieval system or transmitted in any form or by any means, electronic, mechanical, photocopying, recording or otherwise, without prior permission in writing from the imprint owner.

First word – Asicale Ekucaleni

This book presents a concise history of the kingdoms that emerged and dominated the territories between the Zambezi river, the Kalahari to the west, the Indian Ocean to the east and the Limpopo river to the south. Various clans including BaKalanga, BaTonga, AmaShona, AmaNdebele, AmaZulu, BaSotho, BaTswana and many others, would emerge at different times, grow into leading polities and respond to regional changes. The present day states of Mozambique, South Africa and Zimbabwe emerged out of these early kingdoms in the Great Zambezi Valley.

The history of the period 900 – 1500 CE is the focus in this first volume. Written first hand accounts, growing findings by archaeologists and most importantly, the recorded oral accounts of our elders, or Traditions, are used to knit together the stories of the peoples, chronicle the kings and queens, observe how beliefs and customs were integral to crafts in sculpture, mining or farming, and locate the trade networks across the region and beyond. We chronicle the origins of the Early Kingdoms of the Great Zambezi from a Southern African perspective.

FIRST WORD – ASICALE EKUCALENI

Last word – Yikhensile – Asante

Without the work of those who came before us, giants in every sense, this would not have been possible. Beginning with the administrative records in 1500 CE, Traditions passed down and recorded by Hlongwane, Van Warmelo, Read, Tracey, Vilakazi, Nyathi, Mutwa; doctoral research by Bhila, Newitt, Liesegang, Moyo, and the outstanding research by archaeologist Beach, Huffman, Chirikure, Pikirayi, Mosothwane, Van Waarden, Manyanga and Pollard – have all contributed to the view we formed. The list is too long to include here but you meet them as you read on. With so many sources to make sense of whist constructing our views, we hope we have not erred on attribution to sources. Any errors are mine. For Tiggs and Becksylue, my two pillars. Thanking Vovo Mpondza and Vovo Chambale, my old pillars.

    Thank you to all.
        Yikhensi yintamo.
            Siyabonga kakhulu.
                Asante sana.

Maps, Genealogy and Chronology 200 – 1500 AD

MAPS, GENEALOGY AND CHRONOLOGY 200 – 1500 AD

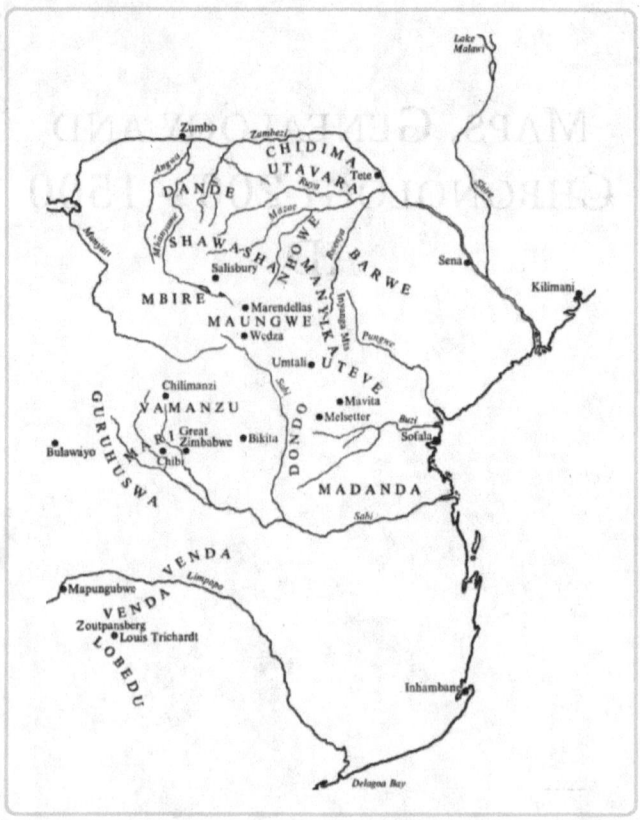

Figure 1: Map of Danda, Teve, Barwe. Manyika, Mbire, Maungwe, Butua and other Mwenemutapa Kingdoms in 1500 CE Lower Zambezi Valley.

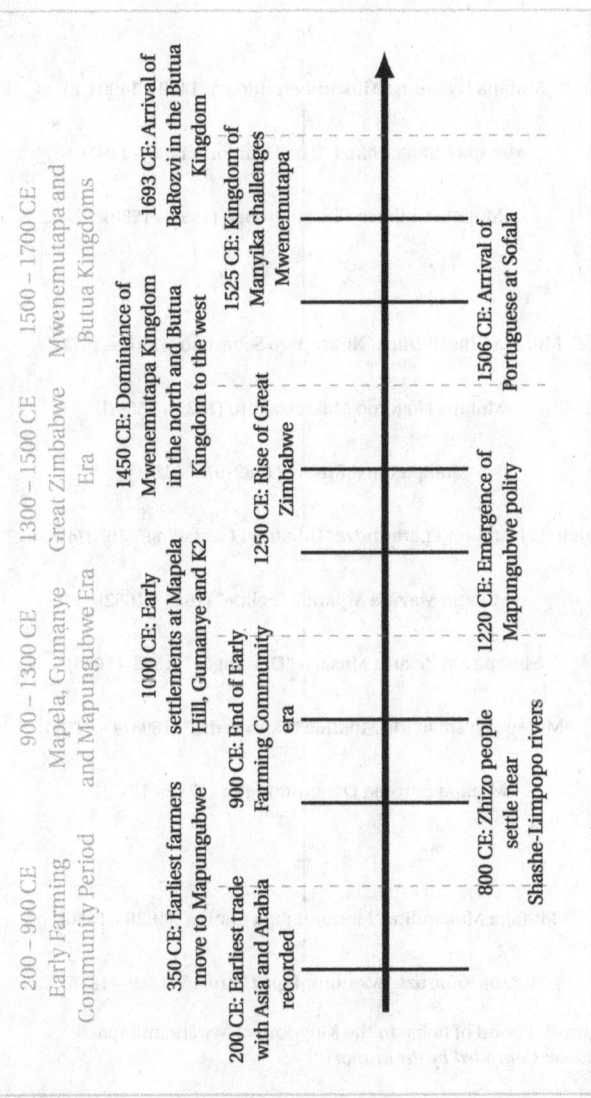

Figure 2: Chronology of the Period 200 – 1700 AD (Compiled by the Author)

MAPS, GENEALOGY AND CHRONOLOGY 200 – 1500 AD

...

Mutapa Nyahuma Mukombero (Reign: 1480 – 1490 CE)

Mutapa Changamire I "The Usurper" (1490 – 1494)

Mutapa Chikuyo Chisamarengu (1494 – 1530)

...

Mutapa Chisamhuru "Xisamparo Sebastiao" (1561 – 1571?)

Mutapa Nogomo Makunzagutu (1571 – 1589?)

Mutapa Gatsi Rusere (1589/97 – 1623)

Mutapa Nyambu Kapararindze "Inhambo Capracine" (1623/4 – 1629)

Mutapa Mavura Mpande "Felipe" (1629 – 1652)

Mutapa Siti Zezuru Musapa "Domingos" (1652 – 1655)

Mutapa Nyamaende Mpande "Dom Pedro" (1693/4 – 1707)

Mutapa Boroma Dangwarangwa (1711 – 1712)

...

Mutapa Mukandira "Monomotapa Candia" (1828 – 1836?)

Mutapa Kataruza "Monomotapa Catruza" (1849 – 1856)

Figure 3: Period of Reign in the Kingdom of Mwenemutapa
(*Source: Compiled by the author*)

"Omi-Ala was a dreadful river:
Long foresaken by the inhabitants of Akure town like a mother abandoned by her children. But it was once a pure river that supplied the earliest settlers with fish and clean drinking water. It surrounded Akure and snaked through its length and breadth. Like many such rivers in Africa, Omi-Ala was once believed to be a god; people worshipped it. They erected shrines in its name, and courted the intercession and guidance of Iyemoja, Osha, mermaids and other spirits and gods that dwelt in water bodies. This changed when..."

–The Fishermen
by Chigozie Obioma, 2015
Published with the kind permission of One,
an imprint of Pushkin Press, London, UK.

MAPS, GENEALOGY AND CHRONOLOGY 200 – 1500 AD

Contents

First word – Asicale Ekucaleni v

Last word – Yikhensile – Asante Sana vii

Maps, Genealogy and Chronology 200 – 1500 AD ix

1 Before the Dawn of Kingdoms in the Zambezi 1
   1.1 Early Settlement Sites 900 CE: Mapela Hill . 7
   1.2 Permanent Settlement: Leopards to the West 14
   1.3 Permanent Settlement: Gumanye to the East 21
   1.4 Kame, Danangombe, Naletale and Manyikeni 23

2 The Kingdom at Mapungubwe 31
   2.1 Rise of Mapungubwe from 1220 CE 35
   2.2 Leadership and Hierarchy at Mapungubwe . 37
   2.3 Conditions for the Decline of Mapungubwe 40

3 The Kingdom at Nzimabgwe 43
   3.1 Kingdom at Great Zimbabwe 1250 CE 51
   3.2 Sacred Worship of Mwari at Nzimabgwe .. 56
   3.3 Rain Making Beliefs and Political Power ... 62
   3.4 BaKalanga: People Of the Sun 67
   3.5 Beads, Ceramics and Pottery 80
   3.6 Nzimabgwe Beyond ist Borders 83
   3.7 Trade on the Coastal Port at Kilwa Kiswani . 86
   3.8 Ivory Route: Sofala, Kilwa, Mombasa and Asia 88

CONTENTS

4 The Kingdom of Mwenemutapa   **93**
    4.1   Nzimabgwe Declines, Mutapa Rises 1450 . .   99
    4.2   Mwenemutapa Kingdom and BaKalanga . . 105
    4.3   The Early Mwenemutapa Dynasty 109
    4.4   BaTonga and BaKalanga Kingdoms 114
    4.5   Mwenemutapa and the New Travellers 118
    4.6   The Rise of the Butua Kingdom 122

5 Various Kingdoms Break from Mutapa   **125**
    5.1   South East of Mutapa: Manyika, Teve, Danda 131
    5.2   Kingdoms South West of Mutapa: Butua . . . 138
    5.3   1500 CE: Scramble and Gibbon Decline . . . 143

Sources in the History of BaKalanga   **147**

Questions in the History of BaKalanga   **152**

Picture Credits   **156**

Bibliography   **158**

1

BEFORE THE DAWN OF KINGDOMS IN THE ZAMBEZI

ANY peoples would have chosen to settle on the hills of Matobo. A crisp morning on the Zambezi Valley, with the sun beginning to lift its head above the horizon. Shimmering dusts of light bounce off the golden spikes of grass that appear to be bowing all they way down the valley, blanketing the landscape as far as the eye can see, interrupted by a path here, a smooth rocky boulder over there or small collection of trees which refuse to grow any taller.

It is bright enough to allow the boys Gwai, Sabi and Sangwe to make their way to the large central *isibaya* where the BaKalanga clan keep their cattle. The households form a ring around one of the mainstays of daily BaKalanga life: cattle herding. Mutapa Mukombero, the leader of all the clans based at the top of the hill, is worried about the upcoming harvest season and the fertility of the lands he has known since he was a boy. Mutapa Mukombero ensures that *Mwari* – the Supreme Being and Creator of BaKalanga

– remains connected to his people, through him, the king. This is a sacred vow and a duty he dedicates himself to wholeheartedly, for appeased gods deliver abundant yields. The Mutapa's existence is predicated on the success of his people, and theirs on their king. Without this vow and the reasons to uphold it, the Mutapa would not exist.

The boys could not have told anyone who asked, which bull belonged to which family in the herd. Each household owned a share of the wealth, whilst paying tribute with their produce, commensurate with yield from the harvest. Different clans and families were known for their specific trade: dry masonry building for some, artisans and sculptors in others, practising medicine as a calling or being the revered as rain makers. At the end of the growing season, mining allowed BaKalanga to walk across the eastern Highlands and sail their *sambuks* down the Zambezi and Save rivers on their way to meet and exchange gold for cloth with travellers at Sofala, Zambezi and Kilwa.

Before the boys could feel the sun on the right side of the cheek, the large herd of cattle had to be grazing beyond the river valley, on the slopes of Matobo, the hills to the west of their village. The hills are named after the granite, *matombo* that erupted to the surface more than two billion years ago to form the existing landscape of large rocks and boulders which provide a viewing point of the valley. On a clear sunny day, the river would be visible from high vantage point. Any peoples would have chosen to settle on the hills of Matobo.

The scene that has been painted takes place in an Early Farming Community, in any of the multiple villages dotted around the Great Zambezi Valley. We want to learn about the various groups forming part of the Early Farming Community; we will follow and live in their stories; we will marvel in their designs and creations; and by understanding their customs and beliefs, we will observe what has been passed down the generations. We want to know how the generations of *Mambo, Changamire, Chibundule, Mpfumo, Inkosi, Induna*, the various kings as they were known, came to acquire power and install their system of governing. Why are rain makers and sacred sites revered? We remove Mapungubwe, Great Zimbabwe and the Mutapa kingdoms from being shrouded in the mysterious romance and mysticism often accorded to the pyramids and Stonehenge. Great Zimbabwe was a lived city, with traditions, industry and trading networks. If Great Zimbabwe is a monument and a sacred site, this is in addition to being the heartbeat of daily life from the 12th century onwards in the region.

Our access to the earliest people in the Zambezi Valley is through their paintings, pottery and earthenware, gold mining and smelting activities, dry stone masonry buildings and various artefacts excavated from the remaining monuments and sites that once formed their homesteads. The people in Matobo and surrounding lands were certainly not the first in this region or beyond. We choose this period as the starting point for this historical account.

We begin the history of Early Kingdoms of Great Zambezi in the latter stages of the Early Farming Community period, which ranges from the year 200 – 900 CE.[1] The earliest peoples who lived around Matombo Hills, referred to as Matobo Hills in modern maps, recorded their daily lives in unique pottery paintings, buried their dead with gold objects, pottery and other valuables. Their remains can be excavated, without intrusion whilst observing the highest standards of conservation, to build an understanding of the cultures, beliefs and interactions of their times and our ancestors.

There are over three hundred sites which were occu-

---

[1] Our notation is BCE for Before Christian Era and CE for the Christian Era or Common Era, more generally known as AD in the Roman calendar convention.

pied by the Early Farming Community.[2] They occupied areas ranging between the Zambezi river to the north, the Limpopo river to the south and Indian Ocean to the east. Archaeologists report that some of these settlements were occupied before 900 CE. The Zhizo people formed part of the Early Farming Community for centuries earlier.[3] We begin in 900 CE, with the history of the Zhizo people and others who came before being beyond our scope.

Matobo Hills lies a few miles south of the present day city of Bulawayo. Place names like Bulawayo are a tapestry on which history is etched. We return to the histories and origins of *Bulawayo* in the instalment covering the period 1500 – 1800 CE. The literal translation of Bulawayo, "where they come to die," does not capture the intended meaning of the name which is: *The Place to be Feared*. Matobo precedes Bulawayo by many centuries. The name *Matobo* retains the meaning that it acquired in momentous times in the 9th century. The Matobo hills bear witness to key historical events in these lands once more, as they did in times past. Some 40,000 years before that, the earliest peoples had settled in these lands and made their mark on Ma-

---

[2] The location and origin of the early farmers remains highly researched and debated. Labelling the period we focus on, 900 – 1500 CE, with the alternative we could have chosen – the Middle Iron Age – presents challenges since the Iron Age period is much wider than that, beginning as early as the 1st millenium BCE. It also creates confusion since in West Africa the Iron Age is a different period. The beginning of ironwork in West Africa is agreed to have begun in the 4th century BCE in present day Yaounde, Cameroon, whilst Rwanda and Burundi exhibit iron muttalurgy from the 1st millenium BCE. We follow the distinction between the Early Farming Community (1st millenium) and Late Farming Community (2nd millenium) provided by JM Morais in 1988. The Stone Age and Bronze Age are so named because of the increased and wide use of stone and bronze tools respectively, over a relatively short period; with 3rd to 7th century for Bronze. The Iron Age covers too wide a period to define it purely based on iron use.

[3] [Calabrese, Interregional Integration in Southern Africa: Zhizo, 2000]. *NB. Note that the full names of sources are provided in the Bibliography; the names of sources on each page are shortened for obvious reasons.*

tobo which would reverberate through time. The paintings found at the *Bambata Cave* depict the daily observations by the people who lived in the same lands 2000 years or more before BaKalanga. The remaining monuments are revered as a site of spiritual worship and respect for ancestors by modern people as it was in the times of BaKalanga. Who were the BaKalanga and the early inhabitants of this land?

We begin this historical journey at similar villages in the Zambezi around 900 CE. Mapela Hill, in the southwestern Lowlands of modern day Zimbabwe, at the confluence of the Shashe and Shangani rivers, revealed wonderful artefacts from excavations by Garlake, Chirikure, Pikirayi and many others. Ceramics, glass beads, spindle whorls for weaving, metal objects, stone walled remains and separated living for the elites are some of findings which are a window into 10th century living at Mapela.[4]

The settlement near the town of Masvingo, known as the Leopard's Kopje or Leopard's Hill, has occupied a pivotal place in understanding of the Early Farming Community. It is no surprise that the town is named *Masvingo*, or "walls of stone," for all around it are various sites exuding history about the people who occupied the area for centuries before. To the northeast near Great Zimbabwe is another settlement displaying its own traditions, culture or style. This district is called Gumanye. The excavations and research from Gumanye Hill revealed that the stone building and pottery style were similar to the observations from Nzimabgwe, or Great Zimbabwe. Mapela Hill, Leopard's Hill, Gumanye and Nzimabgwe have been studied by various teams of archaeologists. They found evidence that the settlements were one of the early sites which were occupied continuously. Permanent settlement, population growth and development of complex societies are of great interest in understanding the emergence of the countries we know

---

[4] [Chirikure, Manyanga, Pollard, Zimbabwe Culture, 2014]

today. We are interested in the inhabitants of Mapela, Leopards Hill or Nzimabgwe. Were the residents of these villages BaKalanga?

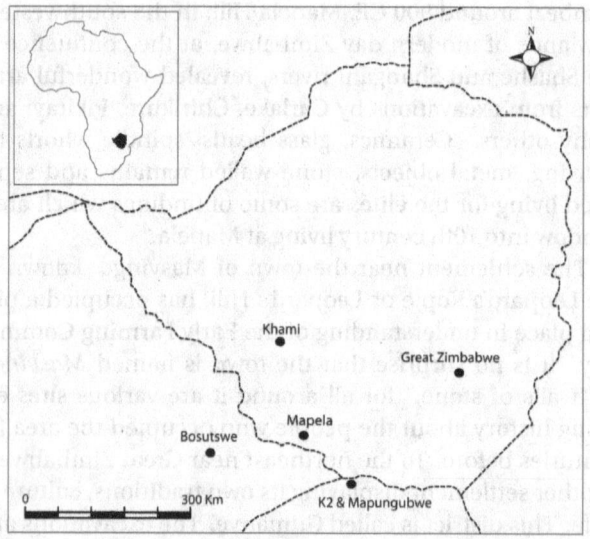

Figure 1.1: The map shows a few Early Farming Community sites where key archaeological evidence has been found: the expertly sculpted Golden Rhino from Mapungubwe, the iconic soapstone birds at Great Zimbabwe or the striking architecture at Khami to offer inspiration.

1.1

EARLY SETTLEMENT SITES 900 CE: MAPELA HILL

OUR knowledge of the Early Farming Community[5] grows with each new excavation, each detailed study made possible by increased resources, and advanced research techniques like carbon dating, satellite imaging and DNA sequencing to mention a few. Holes in the ground are no longer the first step for archaeologists when they learn about the inhabitants of these lands in 900 CE.

New findings are viewed in the context of existing theories and new evidence. Where necessary previous understanding is updated or completely discarded. This has led to textbooks from human origins, to the first settlers in the Zambezi Valley and to the migrations in Southern Africa requiring rewriting again and again. The "Great Lakes Theory" is one increasingly contested view: instead of a single grand and universal narrative, competing views led by the evidence are being put forward. Our understanding of the various changes and complex interactions is evidence led, whilst being comfortable with silent periods in history.

Part of the expansion in knowledge is due to luck in finding enclosures like caves with remains that allow a view into thousands of years ago or melting ice caps revealing well preserved remains. News headlines announce the discoveries: "Lucy, Our Ancenstor !" after the archaeologist dig-

---
[5]The Early Farming Community period covers the years up to and around 900 CE

ging in Ethiopia found inspiration while excavating by listening to the Beatles song "Lucy in the Sky with Diamonds." Announcements include: "Ardi !, Move over Lucy" after another fossil hominid from the Awash region in Ethiopia is found. And, from South Africa's aptly named Rising Star Cave: "Its the Cave that Keeps on Giving: Meet Naledi." Dating to at least 236,000 years ago, Naledi was found with three other hominid specimens by Lee Burger and his team in 2013. We learn of new research undertaken with new findings reported constantly. The findings serve to expand our knowledge of the origins by updating what was known up to that point.

For as long as people have walked on earth, all the evidence points to peoples being present between the Zambezi and Limpopo plateau. The naming of *Zambezi* reflects the reverence for the mighty river and the interactions formed by the early people who dominated and settled near the river. The modern name of Zambezi has evolved from the old *Kasambabesi*, meaning "those well versed with the river can bathe in it."[6] The Zambezi river is highly seasonal and changes yearly on its way to the Indian Ocean. Well known shallow areas and river banks can disappear and new channels take hold closer to the mouth. The river was a revered natural landmark together with the mountains surrounding the villages. The Maravi people defeated the Portuguese in 1571 when Barreto made his first attempt to reach the Mwenemutapa Kingdom via the Zambezi river through Sena. The superior knowledge of the river, its choke points and warfare of the Maravi gave them an advantage.[7]

When trying to date the earliest peoples on the Zambezi Valley, we turn to archaeological evidence of known hominids, ancestors of modern man, that once roamed the plateau. Morocco and Tanzania have pushed back the date

[6] [Pathisa Nyathi, Zimbabwe's Cultural Heritage, 2005]
[7] [Newitt, A History of Mozambique, 1995], p.57

of the previously known lifetimes of the first fossils. The oldest fossil, a skull dating 300,000 years old, was found in Morroco, but there is far more evidence in South Africa of more complete fossils dating to 260,000 years ago. South Africa is not *the* cradle of humankind but one of the cradles of humankind. Rightly, new research covers all areas for the story of beginnings.

We find and present histories to taper the reliance on the views founded on the "single point of origin" story. These views have been widely believed and retain homes in many minds. Following the Kingdoms of BaKalanga and other peoples of the Lower Zambezi Valley will highlight the multiple histories of peoples. As the VhaVenda saying goes, "a stranger may prove to be a relative" once the history has been acknowledged.

The understanding of the Early Farming Community, how they settled at different sites and built indigenous states of the time with recognisable political structures occupies two camps. The earliest research from the first camp which can be engaged as scholarship, proposed that the settlements at various sites of the Leopard's Hill cluster, was where a kin based society emerged, followed by an elite based one at Mapungubwe. And when that society and culture fell into decline it was to the benefit of Nzimabgwe or Great Zimbabwe which rose to prominence around 1250 in the region.[8]

More recent research from the second camp has challenged that old view. The radiocarbon dating of Mapela Hill as early as 1055 CE shows that it was occupied earlier and developed separately.[9] The predecessor settlement to Great Zimbabwe is likely Gumanye, rather than Mapungubwe. The decline of Nzimabgwe coincides with the rise of Mutapa to the north and Khami to the western plateau, with the debate to prove their interconnection being the

---

[8] [Huffman, Mapungubwe and the Origins of the Zimbabwe Culture, 2000]

[9] [Chirikure, Manyanga, Pollard, Zimbabwe Culture, 2014]

BEFORE THE DAWN OF KINGDOMS IN THE ZAMBEZI

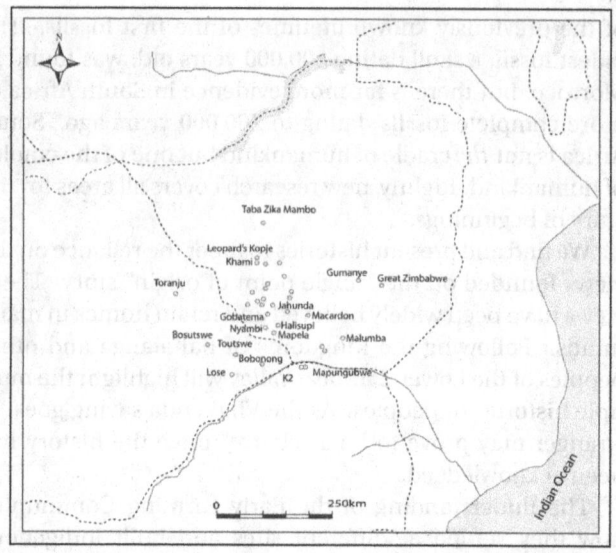

Figure 1.2: The map shows the location of various Early Farming Community settlements, with more than 300 to be found in the Botswana, South Africa, Zimbabwe and Mozambique.

forefront of research.

Archaeologists Chirikure and Pikirayi show that the settlements of the Early Farming Community developed independently, rather than one being a continuation of another.[10] Their study focused on the Mapela Hill remains, on the confluence of the Shashe and Shangani rivers, a site which has been neglected partly due to the difficulty in accessing it, partly due to the status afforded to more popular sites like Mapungubwe.

Mapela Hill is situated on a hilltop with features that exhibit the class distinction found on other settlement sites

---

[10] [Chirikure, Manyanga, Pollard, Zimbabwe Culture, 2014]

EARLY SETTLEMENT SITES 900 CE: MAPELA HILL

of the region: elite buildings on higher ground surrounded by dry stone walls, with commoners living lower down the flat areas down the valley. A fitting description of the scene one would find, with royal households and the inhabitants dwellings, is provided by the novelist Zakes Mda in *The Sculptors of Mapungubwe*. Mda describes the setting at Mapungubwe, 80km to the south east of Mapela, but his description could apply aptly to Mapela Hill, "The commoners counted years in harvests and droughts, the patricians on the hill counted them in kings."[11] Most of the sites share characteristics which we will consider.

Fieldwork from Professor Shadreck Chirikure and his team shows that Mapela Hill is larger than the other well known sites like the Leopard's Kopje K2 site or the Leopard's Kopje Mapungubwe site, both in the south of the hill or kopje. And, having been dated at 1055 – 1400 CE means that Mapela precedes the height of Mapungubwe which dates between 1220 – 1290 CE. With the presence of stone walls, *dhaka* floors made of sand clay plaster, and class distinction called "cultures" by archaeologists, this means Mapela has to be viewed anew. How do the new findings fit with what was known?

The consequence is that Mapungubwe cannot remain the centre where the culture emerged, as previously widely understood. New information from research must be incorporated to revise prior knowledge. In his own words, Chirikure concludes: "Mapungubwe cannot no longer be regarded as the sole cradle of the Zimbabwe Culture."[12]

---

[11] [Mda Zakes, The Sculptors of Mapungubwe, 2013]

[12] Culture for archaeologists refers to archaeological properties and characteristic behaviours identifed from excavations and studied evidence materials. The *Zimbabwe Culture* constitutes class distinction, sacred leadership and cattle accumulation, to list a few markers, as identified by Thomas Huffman. When these characteristics are found in various geographies, the ancient settlement is said to exhibit a similar culture, which is evidence for spatial organisation separating elites from commoners and the development of various crafts including mining, agriculture and trade.

BEFORE THE DAWN OF KINGDOMS IN THE ZAMBEZI

Chirikure's findings at Mapela Hill challenge the "linear framework" of understanding how the early cultures in the Lower Zambezi Valley developed, as proposed by Thomas Huffman.[13] The linear model assigns three phases to the development of societal hierarchy, leadership and commerce: Mapungubwe phase (1220 - 1290), Great Zimbabwe phase (1250 - 1450) with a branching off for Mutapa, and the Khami phase (1400 - 1683).[14] Conferring a privileged position to one archaeological site without detailed research from neighbouring sites has resulted in a narrow and misinformed view of the history. There are more than three hundred of these sites which change our understanding about the Early Farming Community. Chirikure writes:

> This entrenched position is, however, problematic because its linearity has caused more important sites to be assumed to be the capitals of the major phases of Leopard's Kopje (Mapungubwe), Great Zimbabwe (Zimbabwe Culture) and Khami (Zimbabwe Culture). As such, archaeologically well-explored places became the theatres of innovation, thereby editing out of historical significance the many sites that chronologically overlap with the so-called capitals.

The early settlements in the region are shown in the map from Chirikure and his team. The importance of the Leopard's settlements remains irrefutable. The evidence from Huffman, Garlake and others showing the emergence of a structure, a defined society seen in stone buildings, an identity possibly inscribed into pottery and finally the separated leadership of kings from commoners is there to be

---

From these cultures, archaeologists can retrace the emergence of complex societies circa 1000 CE or earlier, with various phases assigned in the academic discpline.

[13] [Huffman, The Leopard's Kopje Tradition, 1974]

[14] The dates provided for the the lifetime of a kingdom, 1400 – 1683 for Khami based Butua Kingdom, will differ from the dates for the materials found and excavated objects from the same site, 1430 – 1650 for glass beads from Khami documented by Pauline Chiripanhura (2018).

EARLY SETTLEMENT SITES 900 CE: MAPELA HILL

examined. Chirikure's new findings point out that there are too many settlements clustered in the same region for the identification of the "first palace, first rain making hill, first gold object, first stone wall..." to be possible, even with advanced measuring and dating techniques.[15] This view could be applied in other spheres outside archaeology where "the first" is used too hastily. In the strict scientific tradition, to claim the first requires proving all others were second or came later. The research so far, which we commend for being meticulous, detailed and ground breaking under enormous challenges, does not yet eliminate other possibilities. This can only be achieved with scale.

The previous work at Mapela Hill had only analysed a quarter of the site which probably affected the findings. Other various sites will get increased research in future which will inform what we know of the Early Farming Community period.

The various early settlement sites also highlight the polities in existence before the emergence of the modern states of Botswana to the west, Mozambique in the east, South Africa and Zimbabwe in the centre. The excavation of thousands of glass beads used in trade provide evidence of exchanges with other nearby kingdoms or directly with traders who travelled to the interior. The archaeological findings establish the links to the Indian Ocean trade route to Sofala and Kilwa Kiswani. Although the Mapela estate is close to a water source, and is within reach of the local gold mines, only copper and bronze objects were recovered by Professor Chirikure and his team.[16]

---

[15] [Chirikure, Manyanga, Pollard, Zimbabwe Culture, 2014]

[16] [Chirikure, Manyanga, Pollard, Zimbabwe Culture, 2014]

1.2

PERMANENT SETTLEMENT: LEOPARDS TO THE WEST

To begin learning about the Early Farming Community[17] by reading the archaeology of Leopard's Hill, a large area also called the Leopard's Kopje, is to begin at the centre of accumulated knowledge about the early societies in the Zambezi plateau. There are numerous early farming communities, more than three hundred, where we could begin.[18] There are even larger, more famous and enduring polities which left behind stirring monuments, magnificent architecture and supernatural sculptures. Great Zimbabwe, the Conical Tower and the Zimbabwe soapstone birds could serve as attractive entry points.

We could have started at the much earlier period of 350 CE when the earliest farmers arrived in the region, or in the period 790 – 850 CE with the Zhizo people, who settled at Leopard's Hill and were known for decorating their pottery. We focus instead on Leopard's Hill after 900 CE because this is where the archaeological data and previous research by Robinson, Garlake, Beach and others, was brought together

---

[17]The Early Farming Community period covers 200 – 900 CE. The location and origin of the early farmers remains highly researched and debated. The beginning of ironwork in West Africa began in the 4th century BCE in present day Yaounde, Cameroon, whilst Rwanda and Burundi exhibit iron muttalurgy from the 1st millenium BCE. Therefore, we follow the JM Morais distinction between the Early Farming Community and Late Farming Community for a clearer nomenclature in this region.

[18][Pikirayi, Great Zimbabwe in Historical Archaeology, 2013]

PERMANENT SETTLEMENT: LEOPARDS TO THE WEST

and expanded by Huffman, Chirikure, Pikirayi, Van Waarden and Mosothwane with countless other scholars, beginning the process of forming a coherent narrative of how the early kingdoms might have emerged. Our aim is to follow the latter period of the Early Farming Community era and construct a clear history of the region from then onwards.

The Leopard's settlement sites point to the early settlers being present in this area for centuries beforehand, which is why we write of the earliest and not the "first". The specific attraction is that the Leopard's settlement offers the earliest archaeological evidence of *permanent* settlement, which is where we begin.[19] The Leopard's site covers a large area now understood in terms of three chronological phrases in the history of the period. Phase I is known as the K2 or Bambandyanalo covering the period 1000 – 1200 CE. Phase II covers the era of Mapungubwe which lasted a few years: 1220 – 1290 CE. And phase III explains the era of Great Zimbabwe 1250 – 1450 CE.[20] The phases track the periods when the settlements were occupied, from which we learn about the peoples of the time using mainly archaeological evidence from buildings, pottery, artefacts and burials. Professor Huffman demarcated the Leopard's sites into two – a northern hill or kopje including the famous Khami remains, and the southern kopje including K2 and Mapungubwe sites.

The Early Farming Community at the Leopard's site created pottery that is distinct from the neighbouring communities. The ceramic styles, called "facies" by the archaeologist Thomas Huffman, are used to identify different groups and the influence they might have had on each other, including movements in the Lower Zambezi.[21] We now know, from the archaeologist Shadreck Chirikure's analysis of Mapela Hill, that Mapela was occupied earlier than the

---

[19] [Huffman, The Leopard's Kopje Tradition, 1974]

[20] [Chirikure, Manyanga, Pollard, Zimbabwe Culture, 2014]

[21] [Huffman, The Leopard's Kopje Tradition, 1974]

Leopard's site. The dry stone walling, which is an important feature for identifying different phases or groups, was built earlier at Mapela Hill (1055 – 1400) than the Leopard's sites (1250 – 1290 for Mapungubwe). Was the knowledge of mining and iron smelting, pottery styling or stone walling skills transferred between the Mapela and Leopard's communities? Each site has been studied in detail and we dive into what is known from latest research shortly. We caution that further research is required to examine how the communities related to each other, as the different viewpoints will highlight. Unsurprisingly, findings from studied sites provide a static history with the dynamic part of events requiring interpretation unless documented.

In addition to the pottery, other artefacts were unearthed from the Leopard's sites including glass beads, shell beads, copper bangles and iron. The trade with neighbouring kingdoms was commonplace. Trade with kingdoms farther afield will be explored from available sources. Evidence of this Early Farming Community also comes from the livestock they kept. Goats, sheep and cattle were kept, with cattle occupying not only the central *isibaya* but their location demonstrated the central role they played in this society. The feature of using cattle to distinguish communities that were cattle keeping, both as a source of food and as a store of wealth, is also well known. The peoples of the Leopards' Kopje have been identified as BaKalanga, occupying areas then now identifiable as northeastern Botswana or western Zimbabwe.

To get a more vivid sense of the Early Farming Community, we jump to an important study revealing more from both the pottery found and the performance of rituals in an importance ceremony – a burial. At the northern Leopard's Kopje, at Mathangwane, archaeologists Catrien Van Waarden and Morongwa Mosothwane observed various practices that associate the settlement site with BaKalanga. A number of bowls, pots and glass beads were buried with

PERMANENT SETTLEMENT: LEOPARDS TO THE WEST

a man – whom we call *Mathangwane* – after his death in the period 1152 – 1212 CE in the upper Shashe river. Eight of the nine pots excavated had been in use well before the burial perhaps for "food and drink prepared in the vessels."[22] The findings provide clear evidence of a ritual burial, but the pots did not have the chevron patterns and other decorations indicative of an elite burial, although a large number of beads were found indicative of wealth. Dr. Van Waarden concludes that the pottery, radiocarbon dates and the glass beads recovered are all characteristics seen in the northern Leopard's Kopje sites. BaKalanga were "likely direct descendants of the northern Leopard's Kopje population."[23]

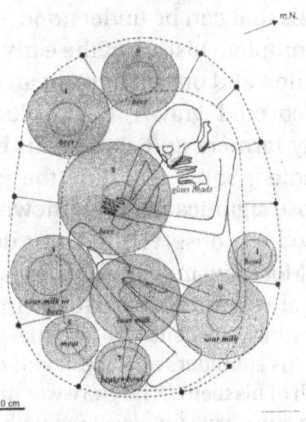

Figure 1.3: Sketch by Van Waarden and Mosothwane of the burial at Mathangwane, in northeastern Bostwana. The burial, pots and jewellery found show the importance of this event with the placing pots and jewellery around the body. Many societies showed similar rituals as Mathangwane man who lived in the 12th century.

---

[22] [Van Waarden, Mosothwane, Leopard's Kopje Burial, 2013]
[23] [Van Waarden, Mosothwane, Leopard's Kopje Burial, 2013]

BEFORE THE DAWN OF KINGDOMS IN THE ZAMBEZI

We get a glimpse into the early settlements people's lives, by studying where they lived and the examining their activities. Understanding their customs, beliefs and societal structures is another piece of the puzzle that will enrich our knowledge. We hope that studying the people and the artefacts which have been recovered, will inform us about their putative views, social hierarchy and the role beliefs played in binding groups together. Crystallisation of beliefs goes hand in hand with population growth in the early societies, as it does to day. That is because cooperation is what binds a people together, creating the conditions for expansion. The archaeological evidence found, projects some of the Early Farming Community beliefs back to us. How an individual is buried, the artefacts and jewellery recovered, and other rituals that can be understood, can all be used to paint a more complete history of the early communities.

The restoration and preservation of archaeological findings from discovered graves are invaluable to learning about the early farmers and settlers in the region. Many have been studied; some revealing the practice of burial with pots, whose significance is unknown. The closest indications come from observing present day customs. Van Waarden and Mosothwane's observations on the burial at Mathangwane are captured in the following key passages:[24]

> His bones have evidence of activities that placed strain on his shoulders and chest, and caused wear and polish of his teeth...The grave was orientated towards the sun's axis, the deceased with his head to the setting sun toward the ancestral spirits...He was laid in the grave wearing a large number of [traded] glass beads, green-blue in colour...unusually high compared to contemporary burials,...probably representing considerable wealth.

There is similarity in knowledge gained from the burial at Mathangwane to a burial from a different period at Sut-

---

[24] [Van Waarden, Mosothwane, Leopard's Kopje Burial, 2013]

PERMANENT SETTLEMENT: LEOPARDS TO THE WEST

Figure 1.4: The nine pots recovered from Mathangwane buried with a man in the 12th century with gold beads are indicative of his wealth. The pottery had residues of beer and red sorghum beer providing a window into the diet of the time.

ton Hoo in England. The lack of knowledge about the Anglo-Saxons living around 616 CE grew the mystery about this period. Following the withdrawal of Romans from Britannia in 410 CE, very little history was recorded afterwards, as writing vanished with the Romans. The excavation of a royal burial in 1939 – what archaeologists would consider yesterday – buried in a ship with a helmet, pots and other artefacts suggested a ritual burial. A previously blank historical era, filled with myths because people always find substitutes, suddenly had real people with customs and rituals presenting themselves for discovery. Research such as seminal paper by Dr. Van Waarden and Dr. Mosothwane add to our knowledge of the people who lived on the Zambezi plateau in medieval times.

Some artefacts which were found at Leopard's settlement have an origin outside the Zambezi or Limpopo valleys. The beads and porcelain found open up a link to the world in the East beyond the Indian Ocean. Anthropologist Marilee Wood and her team show that it is possible that the glass beads were made in Southeast Asia and others came from the Persian Gulf region, forming two distinct networks.[25]

With so many remains of villages of the Early Farming Community, it is not surprising to find that people of the era chose to build settlements near rivers. Sites near the rivers Shashe, Motlouse, Tati have yielded artefacts which date to this period. We have seen that rocky boulders with elevated platforms or hills which allowed a wide view of the landscape were preferred. In Botswana, the villages at Sololwe, Nyangabwe or Ridimpitwe Hill have the same characteristics of the period: stone walling, separated living or cattle farming. Ceramic styles are used to trace and follow the movements of these early communities by archaeologists.

Rituals and a culture projected by discovered burials, which was assumed to have developed much later, have been shown to have been already in use by residents in the Leopard's settlements by 1152. In separate research work, Tawanda Mukwende at the National Museums and Monuments of Zimbabwe showed that the inhabitants of Khami, a Leopard's Kopje site, can be reconstructed from Oral Traditions of BaKalanga and the communities descended from them.[26] The use of dry stone walls and separated living of elites on top of the hill from the commoner down the valley are all seen as features that could be BaKalanga. The similarity in pottery styles, thought to have been created by BaKalanga, does not fully enable scholars to uniquely identify the groups.[27] More research into the movements of people around this period will provide the crucial evidence of links.

---

[25] [Wood et al., Zanzibar & Indian Ocean Trade 1000 CE: Glass Beads, '17]

[26] [Mukwende, The Archaeology of Khami and the Butua State, 2020]

[27] [Chirikure, Manyanga, Pikirayi, Pathways of Sociopolitial Complexity, '13]

1.3

PERMANENT SETTLEMENT: GUMANYE TO THE EAST

WEST of the celebrated Nzimabgwe World Heritage Site, are the remains of another settlement dating to a period even earlier than Nzimabgwe (1250 – 1450 CE). Gumanye (1000 – 1200 CE) is slowly finding its position at the heart of our understanding of the Early Framing Community period.

The previously established understanding from archaeologists was that Leopard's Hill (1000 – 1250 CE) was followed by Mapungubwe (1220 - 1290 CE) with the height of era being at Nzimabgwe. Stone walling, elite burials at the top of the hill, cattle keeping, decorated pottery and the social distinction of the ruling elites, all form part of the characteristics that archaeologists use to understand the inhabitants of the various sites.

New research has provided an alternative sequence to understand which peoples occupied which sites from the 10th century to the 15th. The other less researched sites are now slowly gaining attention, adding to knowledge that can be pieced together. Gumanye is at the centre of this new knowledge together with findings from Mapela. Archaeologists Chirikure, Pollard, Pikirayi and others contend that Gumanye (1000 – 1200 CE) was probably followed by Nzimabgwe (1250 – 1450 CE) before the emergence of Mwenemutapa (1450 – 1800 CE) to the north of Nzimabgwe and contemporaneously the Butua Kingdom (1450 – 1800 CE) to the west.

> **Nota Bene (NB); Buka Kahle (BK):** Standard language to be used for peoples, languages and territories:
>
> **The name of the people** belonging to a single identifiable group have the prefix "***baka-***" or simply "***ba-***" which can be written as "***va-***"
>
> **Their common language** has the prefix "***si-***" or ***xi-*** or even ***tji-***"
>
> **Their home, settlement or the lands** belonging to a single group of people has the prefix "***ka-***"
>
> The People of the Sun, as their name can be translated - **Ba**Kalanga - are the people who settled in the Great Plains below the Zambezi river around 900 CE or earlier, and came to speak **Tji**Kalanga, which is still spoken today. The lands of the People of the Sun, their home, is **Ka**Langa. We capitalise the first letter everywhere. Variations of the descriptions above exist of course.

Leading the new evidence is research into previously under-appreciated historical sites. When the archaeological dating falls out the linear view of how the societies developed, previous knowledge requires evaluating. The pottery style from Gumanye is comparable to that which emerged at Nzimabgwe rather than Mapungubwe. And excavations from a later period offer evidence of Mwenemutapa's similar culture with Nzimabgwe.

We know that the Leopard's Hill peoples were BaKalanga and the culture is observed in various characteristics like dry stone walls, pottery and cattle herds. The peoples of Gumanye were also BaKalanga. All that remains is to provide evidence that the peoples of Nzimabgwe included

BaKalanga. We also know that in the later period of Mutapa, Mambos, Chikangas and Changamires, kings of the various kingdoms of the 15th century, the BaKalanga formed part of either the ruling elite or part of the population in the kingdom.

1.4

KAME TO DANANGOMBE THEN TO NALETALE; AND MANYIKENI IN THE EAST

THE Early Farming Community villages and capital sites were spread between the northern escarpment bounded by the Zambezi river and lowlands surrounding the Limpopo river. The various sites share some similarities with the Leopard's Hill site – stone walling, elite burial, cattle keeping – where a structure to studying and understanding this period was first proposed. Archaeologists call the distinctive features of each sites "cultures."

In modern day Botswana, the early settlement sites include Domboshava, Tati, Toutse, Tsamaya, Kombani, Selokwe, Soswane, Motloutse, Majaneng and many others. Domboshava is famous for its rock painting and remains an active archaeological site.

The closest site to the Indian Ocean is Manyikeni, Mozambique. It has been attributed to the early peoples who migrated eastwards after leaving the Nzimabgwe based kingdom. They went on to build a similar culture and adopted the same style of stone masonry walling surrounding their homes. The walls have been shown to separate the elite rulers up on the hill from the common inhabitants down the valley. Peter Garlake excavated Manyikeni and suggested that it could be the lost capital of the Kingdom of Gwamba.[28] The remains of buildings found on the site today date more than 500 years ago. That the site is similar to Nzimabgwe has been demonstrated through the stone walls, separated living, cattle herding and trade in gold and beads. The word *Nzimabgwe* can be translated as "royal court enclosed with stone," according to Ndzimu-Unami Moyo. Nzimabgwe is taken from the Kalanga language and refers specifically to the enclosures and walls built with stone.[29]

Manyikeni was occupied over two phases. Initially around 1000 CE according to archaeological dating. Manyikeni appears, in a second archaeological dating of the remains, to have been inhabited after 1250 CE until the close of the 18th century. Both the Oral Tradition[30] and archaeology studies strengthen the link between the observed cultures in the region. The connection to Nzimabgwe is palpable: similar dry stone walling, in the same shape, and an apparent elite or royal enclosure. Manyikeni

---

[28] [Garlake Peter, An Investigation of Manekweni, Mozambique, 1976]

[29] [NdzimuUnami Moyo, The Rebirth of BuKalanga, 2012], p.23

[30] Oral Tradition or simply Traditions, refers to testimony tarnsmitted by word of mouth from one generation to another. Various medium are used for storing, enriching and passing information. Songs, poems, theatre, beliefs, practices, customs and many other media are used to capture knowledge. Historical evidence collected through interviews and other oral accounts, have been recognised as invaluable to corroborate, and improve recorded evidence in documents, letters or first published works of history. This is particular important in societies where the motive of some recorders leaps off the page for the readers, leaving a misguided (for believers), uninformed (for rejectors) or shallow view of the same history the chronicler claims to be recording. The question of whether *Traditions* preserve historical facts is addressed by numerous expert scholars in that field including SE Hyman who reviews links between folklore, rituals and history.

was probably a tributary state that we do not find in the administrative records of chroniclers based to the east in 1500 CE. Perhaps it thrived in the earlier period.

The name *Manyikeni* means, "the place of trade." The glass beads that were found, are the archaeological link of Manyikeni to the Nzimabgwe culture. Amongst many recovered artefacts, are three wrought iron objects which were handed to the Swedish Central Board of National Antiquities for analysis. The objects were a spearhead, a gong and a large loop. The gong was interpreted to be a representation of power which reflected the high prestige of its owner. All three metal objects were dated between late 15th to mid 16th centuries.[31] Manyikeni was abandoned in 1700 and only rediscovered in the 20th century.

Most of these Early Farming Community sites are concentrated in the central valley above the Limpopo river and bounded on the east by the Save river and Mount Nyangani. Kame (1450 – 1800), Danangombe (now known as Dhlodhlo) and Naletale (1500 - 1650) are sites of great archaeological interest in the central valley. They were all once ruled by the Torwa dynasty. The nature of the links continue to be studied with more evidence required to buttress the view that Kame was settled first before the move to Danangombe some 120km away, and later Naletale by the same people. Nzimabgwe, or Great Zimbabwe to the east, near the source of the Save river, is known as the best preserved site of a royal court from this period. Naletale has the most magnificent decorations including the herringbone pattern. Chevron decorations feature prominently at various sites as shown in the included photographs.

On the southern banks of the Limpopo river, which is part of South Africa today, the key sites of Mapungubwe and Thulamela have yielded some of the best archaeological findings of the period. We know all about Mapungubwe's

---

[31] [Sinclair PJJ et al., Analyses of slag, iron and ceramics..., 1988]

BEFORE THE DAWN OF KINGDOMS IN THE ZAMBEZI

(a) Dry stone wall at Manyikeni

(b) Dry stone wall at Khami

(c) Dry stone wall at Naletale

(d) Stone wall at Nzimabgwe

Figure 1.5: Remaining monuments of villages, settlements and royal courts in the old kingdoms of the Lower Zambezi Valley. Various clans and groups went on to develop independent building methods and styles, having inherited an approach that was widely used in the region. The chevron style is more prominent at Manyikeni and Naletale.

golden rhino, golden sceptre and golden bowl. Thulamela adds to the evidence of the early settlers. The earliest pottery recovered from Thulamela has been dated to 1240, with gold and ivory showing the extent of activity and trade of the settlers.

Gold beads, gold wire, gongs and a potsherd of molten gold were found in a fortification which probably accommodated more than a thousand people. Like Mapela Hill, or Great Zimbabwe, Thulamela appears to be the centre with various surrounding dwellings in the landscape. The usual structure of separated housing is present. In its heyday, even two thousand people could have lived in the area.

Thulamela, "the place of giving birth" in TshiVenda, probably captured the aspirations of its inhabitants when they settled in this new land. The VhaVenda people remain a recognisable nation with their own language and culture today. Their history can be traced back to the early BaKalanga groups. The Oral Traditions of VhaVenda celebrate their BaKalanga ancestry and they are one of the BaKalanga clans who have retained their identity and went on to forge a modern nation. Today VhaVenda are part of the Republic of South Africa in the continuous process of history that never waits for any particular peoples.

Thulamela is an important site for the proof of metallurgy it has provided. Archaeologists found iron tools, spinning whorls and sewing needles. Metal was being smelted in large quantities this region. The gold jewellery was locally made with signs of trade provided by the Chinese porcelain recovered from the site. The connection to Nzimabgwe is evident but we do not have information to confirm who the people of Thulamela were. In today's map, Thulamela demonstrates the shared ancient history and sits where the borders of the three states to emerge meet: Zimbabwe, Mozambique and South Africa.

Some of the archaeological sites were settled permanently. Owing to their proximity and similarity in pottery styles, encourages researchers who propose that the early peoples moved from one site to another over the years, due to deteriorating climate conditions in one area. There is no universal agreement among archaeologists and anthropologists on this view, although the rainfall data supports the climate change impact. With low rainfall, failing crops and dry grazing lands, it takes no grand theory to understand events of the day. As it can normally be the case, other events could have intervened: nomadic tradition, leadership challenges or external conflict.

The debate to understand how the early peoples migrated, if at all, is centred on the view that inhabitants of Mapungubwe (1220 – 1290 CE) moved to Nzimabgwe (1250 - 1450 CE), and years later their descendants moved to Kame (1450 – 1683 CE), by then the capital of the Butua Kingdom ruled by the Torwa dynasty. This explains the confusion by the Portuguese with the kingdom's name, frequently referred to as "Butua-Torua." [32]

> *Seja como for, talvez devido ao esgotamento dos recursos naturais, a unidade politica de que tratamos entrou em declinio na segunda metade do Sec. XV. Cerca de 1500 a sua capital encontrava-se praticamente abandonada. Como veremos, o seu verdadeiro sucessor foi o Estado de Butua-Torua, a ocidente, com o capital em Khami, no centro de uma regiao com abundantes recursos em agua, solos e pastagems e, para cumulo com ricos jazigos auriferos.*

Rita-Ferreira's extract from the 16th century letters confirms that the capital had been abandoned, perhaps due to lack of natural resources. The residents had moved to a new capital at Kame, where there was abundant water resources, fertile land and the possibility of continuing the

---

[32] [Rita-Ferreira, Fixacao Port. e Historia Pre-Colonial de Mocambique, '82]

mining of gold from new mines.

The residents appear to have moved when conditions dictated in the case of Kame. The proposed view that clans moved from one site to the next generally requires further evidence throughout the Limpopo valley for that assertion to hold. Certainly, some residents of Nzimabgwe ended up in the Butua-Torwa Kingdom before a further move to Kame. This view cannot be generalised for all sites.

The approach we have taken relies on presented evidence. Where it exists, knowledge develops. Where it is contradictory to what we knew before, we discard old views and salvage the useful parts. History is not strange to this process of constant evaluation and construction of new histories. The process guarantees that knowledge marches forward.

There are two competing views that have been put forward to understand the development of cultures from the Leopard's Hill, Gumanye, Mapungubwe, Nzimabgwe, Kame and other sites. Thomas Huffman's view is that the cultures observed at the Leopard's K2 or Bambadyanalo site (1000 – 1200 CE) were expressed at Mapungubwe (1220 – 1290) and later at Great Zimbabwe (1250 – 1450). Shadreck Chirikure contends that the progression was not that sequential. Mapela Hill is the older settlement in the region which could have preceded even Mapungubwe before Great Zimbabwe came into its pomp.

2

THE KINGDOM AT MAPUNGUBWE

WHILST not certain about the origin of the name *Mapungubwe*, the meaning provides a fleeting glimpse of what the first settlers may have encountered on the banks of the Limpopo river. In TshiVenda, spoken in South Africa and Zimbabwe today, Mapungubwe means "the place of many jackals."

The Middle Age settlement at Mapungubwe was known to the present day families living on the Limpopo valley. The sacred site had remained what it was: revered, sacrosanct and undisturbed to appease their ancestors. It has always been a sacred place to the villagers. They knew the source of all the gold – literally and figuratively. The rich history of Mapungubwe told the villagers who lived near it not only about the people who inhabited Mapungubwe in ancient times, but their contemporary lifestyle and beliefs could be traced back to similar beginnings. Things remained the same for centuries. That was until new settlers arriving in the area requested to know the source of a ceramic container they were offered water in.[1] Golden beads, bangles, thousands of ceramics pots and sculpted artefacts were all found on the same site.

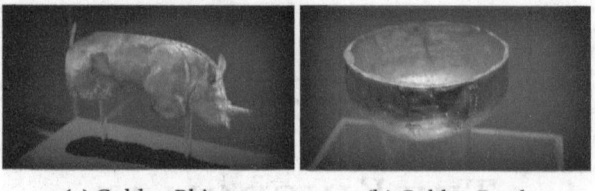

(a) Golden Rhino   (b) Golden Bowl

Figure 2.1: Exquisite artefacts were recovered in 1933 from Mapungubwe: the Golden Sceptre, Golden Bowl and Golden Rhino dated to the 13th century. The Golden Rhino is today an emblem that sits proudly as a symbol of imagination, craftsmanship and wealth, and appears on various South African state institutions' coat of arms. The sculptor Henry Moore was inspired by African sculptures and understood when he stated, "You can learn the history of art...by looking at what has been done in the past...to point they way..."

The archaeological findings from Mapungubwe are some of the most spectacular artefacts from the Early Farming Community period. The excavation of the royal cemetery at Mapungubwe produced a stunning golden rhino that has become a focal point in discussions about the Early Farming Community in the Limpopo basin. The Mapungubwe Golden Rhino has become famous, with the Republic of South Africa naming its highest civilian honour - the Order of Mapungubwe - after the ancient Limpopo based kingdom. The Golden Rhino is the emblem that sits proudly as a symbol of imagination, craftsmanship and wealth. It appears on various state institutions' coat of arms

---

[1] [Carruthers, Mapungubwe: Historical & Contemporary Analysis, 2006]

to preserve this history and project it. A few kilometres to the east of Mapungubwe, the borders of the modern states of Zimbabwe, South Africa and Mozambique would come to be demarcated following their own complex historiography.

Among the many objects recovered at Mapungubwe, three are the most prized: the Golden Rhino, the Golden Sceptre and the Golden Bowl. The sculptures are best preserved and most expertly crafted artefacts found in the Limpopo basin. Carbon dating shows that Mapungubwe was occupied for a relatively short period, between 1220 - 1290. For a long time, the understanding was that the site was abandoned at the end of the 13th century when Mapungubwe lost favour to the emerging state at Nzimabgwe.[2]

This idea of a transition from Mapungubwe to Nzimabgwe has been challenged by new research showing that the kingdoms emerged independently with a separate cultures. This is not to say Mapungubweans never moved, but the generalisation which has been the default understanding is being challenged by accumulated evidence. Professor Chirikure and his team show the stone walled terraces at Mapela Hill were constructed in the 11th century, more than a century before settlement at Mapungubwe.[3] There is no consistency in the view of inhabitants moving from settlement to another. This results in Mapela Hill, an earlier site, being left out. No explanation is offered for the other various sites in the region, or how they fit in this transition.

Mapungubwe remains one of the most active archaeological research sites today. School curriculum have been updated and the public is increasingly informing itself about this period in history. Historians and enthusiasts are keen to preserve and promote the knowledge of the earli-

---

[2] [Huffman, Mapungubwe & Great Zimbabwe: Origin of, 2009]

[3] [Chirikure, Manyanga, Pollard, Zimbabwe Culture, 2014]

est societies between the Zambezi and Limpopo rivers. We learn about mining and smelting methods of the people of Mapungubwe, we discover their sculptors and we can study how societies evolved through beliefs including rain making. The association of kings with divine powers appears in the history of most early societies.

What is not under question about Mapungubwe, is the growth of the population leading to what can be viewed as one of the first towns with the supporting surrounding villages. Population growth is almost everywhere supported by reduced conflicts, expansion in economic activity probably led by an innovation. The agricultural revolution increased food production. This allowed human resources to be allocated to other endeavours other than food.

The industrial revolution added the same spark to economic then population growth. The expansion in the population of Mapungubwe was probably driven by improvements in farming, iron, gold and copper smelting, and the growth of a trading society. More than 26,000 glass beads were found at Mapungubwe in one burial site.[4] We now know that glass beads were used both as gifts and traded with cloth in exchange for gold and ivory.

---

[4] [Wood M., Glass Beads & Pre-European Trade Shashe-Limpopo, 2005]

2.1

Rise of Mapungubwe from 1220 CE

THE settlement on the river banks where the Limpopo river meets the Shashe is the most exciting archaeological site in the region today. The excavation of the Golden Rhino, the Golden Bowl and Golden Sceptre indicated a royal household and led to further findings. Further work on the site has led to understanding of how class and hierarchy probably emerged in the Early Farming Community.

The archaeologist Huffman describes a class-based society emerging from the previous kin-based society at Mapungubwe driven by wealth.[5] He proposed that the expansion in trade allowed Mapungubwe to grow and accommodate a large population. The BaKalanga chronicler NdzimuUnami Moyo estimated the population was probably larger than 5,000 at its peak.[6] Professor Innocent Pikirayi found that the elaborate complex could support a population of up to 18,000 inhabitants.[7] The concentration in one area with the increased coordination between the people whose lives were becoming more linked helped the emergence of societal structures. The emergence of a hierarchical society is assumed to have been the result of these conditions. As always in such studies, we have the evidence of the structure and possible causes but we cannot observe

---
[5] [Huffman, The Leopard's Kopje Tradition, 1974]
[6] [NdzimuUnami Moyo, The Rebirth of BuKalanga, 2012]
[7] [Pikirayi, Great Zimbabwe in Historical Archaeology, 2013]

these directly, for example in writing.

The early inhabitants of Mapungubwe consisted of various groups including *BaKalanga, BaNambiya, Batua-Mambo, BaSarwa, VaNdau* and many others. BaSarwa[8] were not fixed to a single territory; they were nomadic people who traded with villages and cities dotted around the kingdoms along the Limpopo basin. BaSarwa believed that the lands belonged to no one and everyone based on to the beliefs and customs of their ancestors. We have come to know Batua-Mambo as some of the early inhabitants of Mapungubwe partly because of their name, which carries the name of the future kingdom. They would centre this kingdom in the north at Kame, and call it the Butua Kingdom. It would not be rare to find kingdoms with a prefix "The People of..." in the name, where the name can be the clan, a river, a mountain or founding fathers.

Our understanding of Mapungubwe is constantly evolving. The stone walled structures and enclosures that the people of Mapungubwe built were separated from the from the rest of the clan. This observation drove Huffman's position that Mapungubwe demonstrated the first elite pattern in social structures. We now know from Chirikure and his team that the Mapela Hill site dates to a period earlier than Mapungubwe. Nonetheless, the central role of Mapungubwe in the development of social hierarchy, wealth accumulation or sacred worship remains.

The society of Mapungubwe thrived and peaked around 1290 CE, with a clearly formed social structure by then. But there is evidence of occupation of the site going back to 900

---

[8] We do not use the name San people and only highlight it here for those who are not aware that the only accepted name for the people of the Kgalagadi is *BaSarwa* as described by Kiema in *Tears for my Land: A Social History of the Kva of the Central Kalahari Game Reserve, Tc'amnquoo* paper published Gaborone in 2010. The etymology of BaSarwa comes from their southern roots in the region, hence "the People of the South" from the word SeSotho word *serwa*. The clan name has begun the process of restoration from undesired past connotations.

CE. The hunter-gatherer evidence points to activity as far back as 12,000 years ago in the area. We focus on the more recent period where we identified artefacts that inform us about events of the day.

In his great epic novel, *The Sculptors of Mapungubwe*, the South African writer Zakes Mda brings the daily lives of the inhabitants of Mapungubwe to life through the central characters of two boys: Rendani and Chatambudzi. The boys enjoy a carefree childhood with Chatambudzi being more naturally talented at most things. The impending separation is palpable. It is obvious that the boys paths will diverge as they grow, with Rendani having official duties to perform as part of the royal family. The trading networks from Mapungubwe through the kingdoms on the Sofala coast upwards to Kilwa are evoked through travelling in dhows, exchange of gold and cotton for cloth and beads.

2.2

LEADERSHIP AND HIERARCHY AT MAPUNGUBWE

THE first king of Mapungubwe was *Tovera Nemapungubwe*. The Oral Tradition informs us that King Tovera united the various clans, who were not culturally homogeneous. Before the groups became VhaVenda, the earliest settlers were known as VaNgoma. The legendary King Tovera continues to be remembered to day by his descendants in KwaVenda. The area VhaVenda

THE KINGDOM AT MAPUNGUBWE

occupy in northeastern South Africa is testament to the longevity they have enjoyed on the southern banks of the Limpopo river, which they have always called the *Vhembe*.

Tovera's had many sons, including *King Dimbanyika* who established his capital where VhaVenda are found to day. One of Dimbanyika's sons, *Murenga Pfumojena Sororenzou*, also known as *Phophi* went on to leave an equally remarkable story as a leader. He reigned as *King Thohoyandou* – whom the town on the south banks of the Vhembe river in South Africa derives its name. *Thoho-ya-ndou*, "Head of Elephant," is the name he took after ascending to the throne.

VhaVenda's origins are BaKalanga. As we have seen from their beginnings, VhaVenda are a united group of clans from different parts of the Early Framing Community. The process of migration and nation building is not unique to VhaVenda. The ethnography of VhaVenda remain highly debated due to the dynamic and long history in the region. As we will discuss, the histories of most other groups are chronicled by the movements of VhaVenda.

We do not share the view put forward by some researchers that a people could be understood and their cultures explained based on observed "single" behaviours like cattle keeping or bridal customs. As time passes, the interaction across communities muddies what is learned by following a single behaviours. Some customs simply pass to new groups. Languages have shortcomings if we use the same criteria. But they still provide a clue to guide our research for more information. The lineage and oral history of a people is encoded in the language. As researchers we observe the process by which languages develop, and even change with new incomers and their contribution. In the previous section, we saw how archaeology, especially in the absence of recorded testimonies, offers insight into the early communities.

The importance of customs remains central to a people

anywhere. We bring caution to the view that a modern custom can inform us about a people's ancestors as a single trait. How unique and independent the practise of a custom is, cannot be easily observed, especially in the past. We cannot ascribe observations from a small clan to larger identities with any certainty. Yet we recognise that a language retains the old knowledge in the language itself.

The key determinant is not the variable used – building style, farming methods, religious beliefs or languages – but the period in which the people lived and how strongly the characteristic matches the communities of that time. "Cultural norms", according to my old Professor Giddens, "are embedded in the social context of daily action."[9] TjiKalanga has different variations depending on where the speaker is today, but the stem of the language remains the same. The common origins remain, inherited or assimilated. Most speakers of TjiKalanga occupy the south and the central west areas of present day Zimbabwe. Mapela, Gumanye, Khami and the other sites we discuss are in the same areas.

The interaction of language and culture can be seen in other societies. The Reformation in 1517, led by Martin Luther, not only separated Protestants from the Catholic church, but formalised the German language when he translated the bible from Latin. This process makes the tracing of beliefs, their impact, the changes in those beliefs and the evolution of language traceable. Other practices that the people of Germania have passed on cannot be accessed independently unless fully recorded.

To use a custom practised by the descendants of BaKalanga to identify the fifteen century people has its drawbacks in the absence of further documented evidence. What is beyond question, is the rise of leaders within the groups at Mapela, Mapungubwe or Gumanye. And their

---

[9] [Giddens Anthony, The Constituion of a Society, 1984]

2.3

CONDITIONS FOR THE DECLINE OF MAPUNGUBWE

CHANGES in climate including failed rains for a number of seasons, the coronation of a new leader or a takeover by another group are normally the likely reasons for a move or expansion to new territory by the Early Farming Community.

Whilst leadership and social hierarchies were emerging at Mapungubwe, we cannot rule out conflicts due to succession upon the death of a leader or king. The recorded history of this period is not detailed to give context for some of the changes we observe. As we will see later when more daily interactions are recorded for BaKalanga and the Mwenemutapa Kingdom (1500 – 1800 CE), dynastic feuding appears to be almost always at the centre of the kingdoms challenges. The appearance of prophets, travellers and traders from distant lands or natural disasters serve only to widen local disagreements.

King Edward, the King of Wessex, whose son Athelstan would unite the whole kingdom, ruled between 899 – 924 CE. Edward had to overcome the challenge of his uncle for the throne. Edward marched with an intimidating force to meet his uncle where he was camped. His uncle fled and joined the Vikings in the north continuing to be a threat to the kingdom. Ascension to the throne by the son of the *Mu-*

tapa was not a guaranteed in BaKalanga either. In 1490 in the Mwenemutapa Kingdom, Mutapa Nyahuma Mukembero died leading to competing succession claims by his son and uncle. Again in the 18th century in the Kingdom of Manyika, the King Inharugue was ousted in 1807 before regaining the throne and ruling between 1818 – 1820 CE.

In Mapungubwe, there is enough evidence pointing to favourable climate conditions which led it to be occupied.[10] The case of the early BaKalanga, their arrival and expansion at Mapungubwe is believed to have been a continuation of their previous settlements at Leopard's site and other similar settlements where conditions later deteriorated forcing the move away from Mapungubwe.[11]

Climate conditions before 1500 have been charted by meteorologists which support the view that the decline in rainfall led to abandonment of Mapungubwe. The actual records we have are for much later in the century including the floods of 1563 – 1565 CE in the Mwenemutapa Kingdom and upper Zambezi discussed by Sousa 1697. Before this, the only other natural disaster recorded in the archives is the drought, locust attack and famine of 1561 – 1563 CE affecting the Mwenemutapa Kingdom as recorded by both Fernandes in 1562 and Sousa in 1697.

---

[10] [Huffman, Climate Change Shashe Limpopo, 2009]
[11] [Van Waarden, Mosothwane, Leopard's Kopje Burial, 2013]

THE KINGDOM AT MAPUNGUBWE

3

THE KINGDOM AT NZIMABGWE REVERBERATES THROUGH THE AGES

DATED to 1250 - 1450 CE, *Nzimabgwe* is a collection of stone walled structures of a magnificent ancient city covering an area of 700 hectares that once dominated the seemingly barren plateau. The landscape is bounded by large granite boulders creating a recognisable landmark of giant whalebacks followed by flat granite hills. From a distance, the meandering valleys drift off the top of the flat hills. About 30km east of Masvingo in the south east of present day Zimbabwe, one of these flat hills, on raised ground relative to the surrounding landscape, was chosen by the early settlers for building of the capital of their kingdom: Nzimabgwe.

Nzimabgwe is the original name of the old kingdom. To day it is known as the Great Zimbabwe National Monument. The word *Nzimabgwe* can be translated as "royal court enclosed with stone," according to Ndzimu-Unami

Moyo. The name is taken from *TjiKalanga*, the Kalanga language, and refers specifically to the enclosures and walls built with stone surrounding the central elite residences.[1]

Most of the building at Nzimabgwe dates around 1250 CE and after. There is evidence that Nzimabgwe was settled much earlier than that. One of the buildings and its floor in the north of the site called the Hill Complex, dates as early as 1100 CE.[2] One of the hard *tambuti* wood timbers which held a doorway was found to have been cut in 600 CE using the radiocarbon dating technique.[3] The Nzimabgwe site is well preserved considering the 800 years it has stood, and the looting it has endured over centuries. The remaining monument at Nzimabgwe displays the high quality of craftsmanship of the stone work, with nothing besides gravity and the architectural precision to hold the buildings in place for centuries. The outer structures of the ancient city of Nzimabgwe still display the magnificence achieved by its 13th century architects and builders.

Inside the city, the layout was set out with purpose and function foremost in mind. Houses, private forums, communal areas, public markets, symbolic towers and the enclosing walls were laid out to separate the different working and living quarters. The layout alone, which remains visible even where the buildings have degraded, provides a clue to the functioning of this society. The archaeological findings from Nzimabgwe provide a rich collection of evidence of a kingdom and a people that thrived 160 kilometres east of the venerated spiritual hills of Matobo. Both Nzimabgwe and Matobo Hills are sites of pilgrimage. They had always received a high number of visitors[4] and worshippers for both their architectural and spiritual significance to their

---

[1] [NdzimuUnami Moyo, The Rebirth of BuKalanga, 2012], p.23

[2] [Chirikure and Pikirayi, Inside and Outside the Dry Stone Walls, 2015]

[3] [BBC Pathe Archives, Buried Treasure: King Solomons' Mines, 1958]

[4] The number of visitors exceeds 100,000 per year according to the Protection of World Cultural and Natural Heritage Sites from UNESCO.ORG

descendants, long before they acquired their new status as World Heritage Sites in 1986.

At the northern end of what was the centre of the kingdom, up on the highest hill of the site at Nzimabgwe, is the Hill Complex with two separated enclosures, the Eastern and Western Enclosures. This part of the Nzimabgwe is the oldest making it the first to be built. It is where the royal residences were located. The king and his closest advisor had their quarters separated from other houses by narrow dry stone walls. Being on this hill created a clear separation from the rest of the residences down the valley. This is one of the most notable characteristics and has led historians to confirm that social hierarchy was already established by the Nzimabgwe era. The Hill Complex is where six columns of upright posts measuring about 90cm hoisting up the soapstone birds were found. The birds are a recognisable and famous symbol of Zimbabwe. The ancient city bequeathed its name and image to the whole country.

Some artefacts have been lost or looted from the site. With the many ancient remains that stand ready to contribute to archaeological knowledge and history, unscrupulous actors match them with purpose to detract from that ideal. Of the eight Zimbabwe birds that once stood at Nzimabgwe and were found, only four can be found at the National Museums and Monuments of Zimbabwe. The four birds were returned by South Africa in 1981. More recently, a fifth bird was returned in 2003 by Germany to Zimbabwe.[5] Posselt wrote about the soapstone birds found at Nzimabgwe:[6]

> Each one, including its plynth, had been hewn out of
> a solid block of stone and measured 4 feet 6 inches
> in height; and each was firmly set into the ground.
> There was also a stone shaped like a millstone and
> about 18 inches in diatemeter, with a number of fig-

---

[5] [Munjeri, The Reunification of the Stone Bird of Great Zimbabwe, 2003]
[6] [Posselt FWT, Fact & Fiction: A short account of Southern Rhod., 1935]

ures carved in the border. I selected the best specimen of the bird stones, the beaks of the remainder being damaged, and decided to dig it out.

The Zimbabwe birds which can be seen on the country's flag are the most famous avian sculptures that have been found in the region. The inhabitants of Great Zimbabwe were not the only society in the region that made sculptures of symbolic figurines. To the west in present day Botswana, three *Vukwe birds* were dug up by the archaeologist Wieschoff in 1929 near Francistown. In a typically disastrous story that you could have guessed before the end of this sentence, the Vukwe birds are now lost having been taken by Wieschoff to Germany. The "clay birds, painted in red and black" dated as early as 1430 CE but have completely disappeared from their Germany storage.[7]

To the south of the hills at Nzimabgwe, on the low planes of the city, is the Great Enclosure, built in an oval-looking shape. The Great Enclosure is surrounded by a 250 metre wall, 10 meters tall at the highest point and 6 metre thick. To give a visual idea, It is said that a small modern car could easily drive on top of the wall. There are three entrances: to the north west and another to the north which leads to the narrow path and towards the Conical Tower. The west entrance appears to have been completely separated from the rest of the enclosure. The Great Enclosure, called *Imbahuru*, was an important part of the royal court for it was "the house of the great woman." It belonged to the Queens of BaKalanga. The Great Enclosure was built from granite rocks quarried locally, and timbers cut from the region. One of the timbers from the Western Enclosure was dated to 1065 CE.[8] Within the series of living quarters, the community area in the middle would have brought the elite residents of the enclosure together, from which a narrow passage leading to the famous Conical Tower was accessible.

---

[7] [Lane, Reid, Segobye, Ditswa Mmung: Archaeology of Botswana, '99]

[8] [Hall and Stefoff, Great Zimbabwe, 2006]

The tower measured more than 22 metres high in its heyday with about 10 meters now remaining. The base is 20 feet (about 6 meters) wide at the bottom narrowing to 10 feet across at the top.[9] It is still one of the most magnificent structures that one can see at the old Kingdom of Nzimabgwe. Was the Conical Tower decorative, a storage unit or did it have any another significance? The reasons for building the tower and its function continues to attract scholarship with no singularly convincing narrative. Views associating the birds with *Mwari* beliefs, in the same way the people of Kemet worshipped and painted the *Ra* the Sun God, have found more traction. We still have no written indications of this. We explore the symbolism of the Zimbabwe birds in the section on Sacred Worship and Mwari. Perhaps, some monuments are built to send a message to future generations. Why does the message remain a mystery to the current generation?

There are numerous peripheral and small walls acting as enclosures for houses down the valley sitting northwards of the Great Enclosure. This area of the lower valley enclosures is called the Valley Complex. A series of *dhaka*[10] houses were spread out throughout the valley. Archaeologically, this area has been the most informative, enabling scholars to study close living among the inhabitants, social interactions, working life and the possibility to estimate population sizes. The estimates of the population range from 5,000[11] to 10,000[12]. The craftsmanship on display in the building work is of a very high standard. The walls clearly separated the living areas but appear to have a decorative function too. The high walls have distinct chequered patterns in different places, with the overt displays

---

[9] [BBC Pathe Archives, Buried Treasure: King Solomons' Mines, 1958]

[10] The houses had walls made of granite stone and a mixture of granitic sand and clay

[11] [Huffman, Mapungubwe and the Origins of the Zimbabwe Culture, 2000]

[12] WHC.UNESCO.ORG

like chevrons creating breaks in the stone work. The building has stood for at least 500 years. if Zimbabwean artifices are looking for inspiration, the old kingdoms are a place to look.

To understand the society in the Kingdom of Nzimabgwe we will need to consider the sources of income. To build and grow a society on this scale required enormous resources. What goods were produced and traded? Gains through trade are required for population growth which in turn contributes to the expansion of the city. Cotton weaving, gold mining and cattle rearing formed part of the numerous activities identified by scholars which we will discuss. Written records will offer insight into the kingdom which had its centre at Nzimabgwe.

We remind ourselves, that there were other settlements at the time Nzimabgwe flourished. Kame, Mapela, Gumanye, Taka Zika Mambo or indeed Mapungubwe could have been trading with the largest kingdom of the time at Nzimabgwe. Chirikure and his team found copper-based ornaments, bronze objects and spindle whorls during the Mapela excavation.[13] Copper, bronze and crucially, cowry shells and glass beads were found at all other sites.[14] Cowry shells and glass beads were used as a means of exchange.

The archaeological findings from the remains at Nzimabgwe are unmatched in quantity and variety of origin. There are prestige goods from India, Persia and China which were given as gifts during royal courtship, or were acquired in trading exchanges. A record of what the exchange would have looked like, but for a period a few decades later, and from Europe is instructive.

The traveller Anhaia, who was stationed at Sofala wrote a letter to his king dated 27 October 1505 "to enter to the account of Manuel Fernandes, factor of Sofala, the gifts made

---

[13] [Chirikure, Manyanga, Pollard, Zimbabwe Culture, 2014]

[14] [House, Archaeology of Mapela Hill, South West Zimbabwe, '16], table on p.28

to the king of Sofala." He proceeds to list cotton, brass pots and a string of blue Venetian glass beads which had five hundred beads, as well as other objects which were offered in the reception with the king.

The Persian bowls found at Nzimabgwe had inscriptions from the 13th century. Other objects found include the Chinese porcelain celadon ware that was dated to the Ming era (1268 – 1644 CE). At Nzimabgwe as is the case in most settlement sites around the Zambezi, thousands of glass beads are always uncovered. Research by Ndoro and many others shows the source to be India and Southeastern Asia.[15] Note that settlement, peak and beginning of the decline of Nzimabgwe dates to the period *before* the arrival of the Portuguese. The Kingdom of Nzimabgwe and the neighbouring kingdoms we explore, had their kings, mined gold and traded for centuries through the Indian Ocean.

Figure 3.1: The famous Zimbabwe soapstone birds recovered from the old Kingdom at Nzimabgwe. Eight birds with both avian and human features found in belief systems of other cultures were found mounted on plinths. Their significance to us or the 15th century inhabitants of Great Zimbabwe has not revealed itself to scholars. BaKalanga have probably always known.

---

[15] [Ndoro, Great Zimbabwe, 2005]

THE KINGDOM AT NZIMABGWE

The soapstone birds recovered from Nzimabgwe are a world famous symbol of the old Kingdom at Great Zimbabwe. The soapstone bird sits on the coat of arms, flag and currency of the modern state of Zimbabwe. Eight soapstone birds, measuring about 30cm were recovered from the remains of Great Zimbabwe; seven from the Hill Complex and one from the Valley Enclosures.[16]

The sculptures present a combination of a real and imagined birds of prey, with both avian and human traits which are yet to reveal their significance. One bird "has lips rather than a beak; all have human limbs and four or five toes or fingers in front rather than three talons like most raptors."[17]

It is thought that the birds went beyond providing an aesthetic function, representing divine kingship and sacred worship. We cannot elaborate with certainty. The Huastec society in Mexico fell to the Aztecs in the 15th century, leaving behind sandstone sculptures with one known as the Huastec Goddess. To understand the meaning of the sculptures of female deities whose most distinctive features are the face and breasts, researchers have to work through filters of languages and peoples who came after the Huastecs: the Aztecs, the Maya and the Spanish. The Goddess is said to have represented fertility and renewal.[18]

The most detailed and persuasive reconstruction of the birds' significance has been offered by Edward Matenga who confirms their sacred status and that "they are an integral part of the spiritual image of Great Zimbabwe."[19] That a hierarchical structure of society had long emerged by the Nzimabgwe era is beyond doubt. One wonders how the birds were viewed by both the healers and rain makers, they royals higher up the hill and the commoners lower down

---

[16] [Matenga, The Soapstone Birds of Great Zimbabwe, 1998]

[17] [Huffman, The Soapstone Birds from Great Zimbabwe, 1985]

[18] [Evans and Webster, Archaeology of Ancient Mexico, 2001]

[19] [Matenga, The Soapstone Birds of Great Zimbabwe, 1998]

the valley. The following myth from BaRozwi is instructive of how natural landmarks or sculptures like the birds formed part of the belief system:[20]

> Their traditions tells us that they were accompanied on their travels by a voice which they called Tovela which led them on their way, keeping them safe from dangerous places. The voice could speak from any object it chose...The voice of a presence whom some say was that of the first Rozvi ever created, the founding father of the clan...Tovela not ony protected his people on their travels but gave them food as well...He also gave them medicines to become invincible but not inaudible to their foes and to be long lived. Tovela came to be called...Mwari.

3.1
KINGDOM AT GREAT ZIMBABWE 1250 CE

NZIMABGWE is the largest, most famous and the best preserved site of the early Kingdoms of BaKalanga. Historians believe that Nzimabgwe was the centre of a larger kingdom from 1250. Certainly, BaKalanga peoples can trace their origins to Nzimabgwe. But, they were not the only inhabitants of the kingdom. There is evidence of other clans who identified as part of the larger BaKalanga identity. The BaLemba, BaLozwi, VhaVenda are all clans of BaKalanga. Were these clans at Nzimabgwe together with other groups who were were not BaKalanga? The confir-

---

[20] [Hodza and Fortune, Shona Praise Poetry, 1979]

THE KINGDOM AT NZIMABGWE

(a) Narrow passage in the Great Enclosure, Nzimabgwe

(b) Artist impression of Great Enclosure, Nzimabgwe

Figure 3.2: The narrow passage in the Great Enclosure at Nzimabgwe viewed from both a recent photograph and an artist's rendering of its heyday. The passage wall leading to the Conical Tower is 10 meters tall with nothing but precision in design and construction holding it in place since the 12th century. This was the House of the Great Queens of Nzimabgwe with the kings quarters located in the Upper Enclosure on the hill.

mation we have is that the groups and clans at Nzimabgwe were BaKalanga. We also know of another group, BaSarwa, who were not BaKalanga but wandered through various parts of the Lower Zambezi Valley without attaching to a single territory. BaSarwa were one of the earliest groups in this region who later settled in the Kgalagadi. Did some BaSarwa settle at Nzimabgwe with BaKalanga?

Archaeology dating has shown that Nzimabgwe or the

KINGDOM AT GREAT ZIMBABWE 1250 CE

Figure 3.3: The Great Enclosure is the most visible remaining building at Nzimabgwe, a World Heritage Site whose origins in the 12th century is but one of the monuments that hold a history of the peoples of the region. Several smaller enclosures can be seen in the foreground. It is estimated that at least 5,000 people lived in the greater area of Nzimabgwe covering 700 hectares.

Great Zimbabwe National Monument, dates to 1250 - 1450 CE. The building began as early as 1100 CE with various sites added over time. The stone walled structures without mortar built more than 500 years ago are still standing today. Nzimabgwe has been declared a World Heritage Site by UNESCO. Various studies have established that Nzimabgwe was occupied by ruling elites living at the top of the hill and commoners lower down the valley.

It would not be until 1871 when an archaeological survey would be conducted by Mauch. Unfortunately for Mauch, and readers many centuries later, he was one of those "scientists" who knew the answers before beginning excavations and research. He let his prior views drive the conclusions in spite of the archaeological evidence in front of him. The view that Nzimabgwe was the long lost Palace

THE KINGDOM AT NZIMABGWE

(a) The Conical Tower   (b) The Main Entrance

Figure 3.4: The Conical Tower in the Great Enclosure and a Main Entrance of the 13th century old Kingdom of Nzimabgwe. The timber poles at the entrance were radio carbon dated to 1065 CE indicating settlement at Great Zimbabwe was much earlier than the conventional period of 1250 – 1450 CE used by scholars to indicate the period it was inhabited.

of King Solomon who ruled from 970 to 931 BCE took seed from Mauch's surveys and early reports. Mauch was probably following a long tradition of searching for gold.

Researchers would continue to study the site over many years. The confirmation of Nzimabgwe having been built by peoples the Portuguese referred to as *Mocaranga*, or BaKalanga if they could spell it correctly, would be indisputable under the weight of documentary, archaeological and Oral Traditions knowledge. Over time, the interior lands between the Zambezi river and the Limpopo river came to be known as Zimbabwe, after the 13th century kingdom based at Nzimabgwe.

The people who lived in Nzimabgwe left behind a variety of evidence to tell their story. Archaeologists have found various earthenware, iron works and ivory which are a window into their times. The peoples of Nzimabgwe and those who came before them weaved cotton, mined and smelted iron, kept cattle and other livestock, worshipped their own gods, built leadership structures and traded with neighbours and foreigners alike. Function did not seem to be the only aim – aesthetic presentation mattered. Continued research at other sites like Gumanye, which is now known to have preceded Nzimabgwe, can only clarify our knowledge of this period in history.

If we move beyond Nzimabgwe and the region, were other people writing about Nzimabgwe? We find references to Zimbabwe from the 1490 writing of the Arab cartographer and navigator Ahmad Ibn Majid who sailed from present day Oman to various ports on the East coast including Mombasa, Kilwa and Sofala. Majid not only describes the navigation required to reach those destinations using stars, latitude reading, finger mapping, but he also paints a mental picture of the villages, their trading activities and the islands dotted around the peninsula including Mozambique Island and Vamizi. Majid writes:[21]

> Concerning Sofala, it is separated from the people of Muna-Musavi (Mwenemutapa), and the ruler of Zabnavi (Zimbabwe), it is here that the gold mines are...Here Zabnavi governs, and in the South there are no others that are equal to him.

---

[21] [Ahmad Ibn Majid, Book of Info. on Principles of Navigation, c.1490]

3.2

SACRED WORSHIP OF MWARI AT NZIMABGWE

BAKALANGA believed in the power of their ancestors and a Supreme Being to guide them through their lives and provide divine wisdom and strength. BaKalanga expressed gratitude for abundant yields in crops or spoke of a better yield in failing years. The Supreme Being they gave gratitude to, and asked guidance from, is the *Mwali* or *Mwari*.

The belief in Mwari was established by the time of Mapungubwe (1220 - 1290 CE). Separately, we know that the belief in Mwari was practised and expanded in the height of Nzimabgwe (1250 – 1450 CE). Evidently, Mwari provided what Harari calls the *Imagined Order*[22] with the kings asserting that any ideas the society believed in – cooperative farming, communal living, paying taxes to an overlord – were a reality created not by the kings, but by the ancestors, nature and Mwari. What are the origins of the belief in Mwari?

BaKalanga believe that the first man was created by Mwari at Matobo Hills, the World Heritage Site near present day Bulawayo. Mwari, the Supreme Being, made the first man *Musikavanhu* in the heavens after which he descended to earth. Musikavanhu had dreams of birds and animals roaming the landscape. A woman appeared and became his wife, from which they are descended. The BaKalanga people believe their ancestors go to *Nyikadz-*

---

[22] [Harari, Sapiens: A Brief History of Humankind, 2011]

imu, the Ancestral Spirit World. Their creator, *Mudzimu*, is called upon by the divine beings in times of need. BaKalanga and followers of Mwari believe their calls are answered to this day. The spirits of the BaKalanga kings are believed to return as lions called *Mhondoro*.

The leaders of BaKalanga were believed to have been bestowed sacred leadership and possessed divine powers including rain making through the consecrated sages. This earned the respect of the common subject and bolstered the reverence and support for the king. A leader depended on the belief of his people in him and the institution of Mwari. The belief in Mwari, BaKalanga kings, their rule and application of law, called *Milango* was so strong that the newly arrived struggled for centuries to introduce foreign religions in the Zambezi Valley. Whether the newly arrived knew it or not, in the sense that they had a strategic plan to introduce a different religion, targeting BaKalanga beliefs would prove incredibly ineffective for millennia. Beliefs have been shown to be at the centre of emergence of complex societies from the Americas to the Levant to Africa.

We know from the Moroccan Muslim explorer Ibn Battuta that he reached the port city of Kilwa in 1330 and other traders had been trading with the Mwenemutapa as early as the eleventh century. Belief in Islam was common on the coastal towns of Mombasa, Kilwa and Sofala. The map of the towns in a famous painting of 1572 provides an impression to a modern day observer from an eyewitness. We get no indication from the records that there was an attempt to introduce Islam into the Lower Zambezi Valley. Most of the correspondence centres around trade, negotiations, markets and more trade.

When the Portuguese first arrived in 1506, they dropped anchor at Sofala and travelled inland see the *Monomomapa* rulers. On that occasion they were not successful and relied on accounts from traders and locals for information. Some years later, they travelled north from the Sofala coast to use

THE KINGDOM AT NZIMABGWE

the Zambezi river as an alternative route inland. Before that trip, the Portuguese built a settlement on the Zambezi coast, at Quelimane, from which they traded continuously with the various dominions in the region before the first foray inland. There are innumerate trade records and letters capturing the diplomatic relations with the Kingdoms of Mwenemutapa, Barwe, Manyika and Teve of the time. The Kingdom of Danda and Butua also appear in the documents in times of conflict with the new travellers.

Christianity was introduced at various times into the Kingdom of Mwenemutapa but failed to take hold due to centuries-old beliefs in *Mwari*. The first time would have been in 1506, when the first Portuguese travellers left Sofala headed to the interior with the bible. Historical records show that for many decades, they failed to attract followers. Around the same time, Islam had only been adopted by a few coastal residents, even though the religion had been introduced many centuries earlier, possibly as early as the 10th century by the early traders from Arabia. Having failed to change local beliefs including *Mwari*, the Portuguese would turn to converting the kings, *mambos*, *mutapas* and *chikangas* first.

Various events take place frequently to be noticed, but once in a while events do occur that shift what the people of the time know or will believe. The changing of the many gods of the people of Kemet to just one, the *Aten* by Pharaoh Akhenaton in 1353 BCE is one such event. The move from Mecca to Medina in 622 CE by the Prophet Mohammed resulting in a completely new date, *Year 1* is undoubtedly another. For an event we are likely to have experienced, the moon landings are possibly the closest in modern history that left a sense of *before* and *after*. In the villages and kingdoms between the Limpopo and the Zambezi rivers, the arrival of Christianity which eventually replaced *Mwari* and other local beliefs had an equally momentous shift. Although the first Mutapa to convert to Christianity was *Mu-*

tapa Gatse Rusere before his death in 1623, at a large scale, BaKalanga would not convert until the arrival of the missionaries in the late 1800s.

"Monomotapa Gatse Lucere", as the sources name him, had reign lasting from 1589 - 1623 as recorded by Beach using Oral Traditions from the area.[23] Mutapa Rusere's baptism introduced an institution that would etch itself deeply into the spirituality of the peoples of the region, permanently replacing Mwari and other beliefs. The Traditions corroborate the administrative records of the Portuguese on Mutapa Rusere's conversion to Christianity. At the time of his rule, the Portuguese had gained a footing in Mutapa leadership structures, influencing Mutapa Rusere to their benefit. Some sources go as far as labelling Mutapa Rusere a puppet until his death in 1623.

Mutapa Rusere's son, Mutapa Nyambu Kapararidze, known as "Capracine" in the archives, succeeded but did not convert as he regained power in the Mwenemutapa Kingdom. We know that he was based at Massapa, the capital of Mwenemutapa in November 1628, because he is mentioned as fighting the Portuguese and trying to remove them from his kingdom.[24] He was evidently trying to regain control after the losses under his father Gatsi Rusere. Mutapa Kapararidze's rule was followed by an eventful period of rule by Mutapa "Felipe" Mavura Mpande between 1629 – 1652 CE. In that period, and as is clear from his given name, Mavura converted to Christianity; he oversaw the famous rebellion of 1631 against the Portuguese; and he presided over the separation in the house of Mwenemutapa into two royal houses. A list of Mutapas with the chronology we have researched and confirmed is included with the photographs and maps. A biography of Mutapa Mavura Mpande alone could fill a few volumes as it captures the pivotal changes in the kingdom that are indicative

---

[23] [Beach, Mutapa Dynasty: Documentary & Traditional Evidence, 1976]
[24] [Pikirayi, Ceramics, Global Networks of Trade and Interaction, 2012]

THE KINGDOM AT NZIMABGWE

of the beginning of its decline. Gibbons anyone?

The events show that worship of Mwari played a role in the keeping back, not only foreign beliefs, but political and legal power within BaKalanga. The Portuguese had tried numerous times to introduce Christianity to replace Mwari belief system without success. By the time the Portuguese were expelled by the King of Manyika in 1590, very few people had converted to Christianity. Saldanha wrote in 1511 of the difficulty in getting through to his king: We "hope that, God willing, the (BaKalanga) will turn Christian and that with them we will throw out the (Muslim) even if they are many."[25]

The success in converting BaKalanga and BaTonga to Christianity largely came when the Portuguese understood the association of sacred beliefs with daily life through the medium of spirituality. BaKalanga worked their land, believed in *Mwari* to deliver rains and trusted the Mambos to act in the interest of the kingdom. From that followed good yields in crops, growth in farm herds, expansion in gold trading and the wealth of the kingdom. Periods of drought, famine, war or plague were not absent, with the farmers looking to their toil, Mwari and the Mambos to deliver better times. The benefits from local beliefs and customs accrued directly to BaKalanga spiritually, and as they believed, materially in various ways. The birth of a child for instance, was seen as a blessing which manifests itself as a gift of a new member of the family. The newly arrived on the coast needed to penetrate and intercede in this cycle.

At a beaucratic level, the people looked to their king and courtiers to adjudicate *milando* – a word which used to indicate a debt of many kinds – but today means the law or justice. The relationship between the rain makers, healers and the king was such that they were viewed as one institution. This was not unique to this society. The different dis-

---

[25] [Barros, Da Asia: Dos Feitos, Que os Portugueses Fizeram..., 1778], Vol. III, p.11

ciplines of astronomy, law, medicine, philosophy or even agriculture would not have been recognised as separable from Christian beliefs back in Portugal in 1500. Christianity came to be widely adopted in the 19th century in the lower Zambezi Valley. BaKalanga did not view social structures as distinct from their beliefs, no more than other societies did. Shared beliefs, customs and common history was what bound the kingdoms together. When the hopes and fears of the kingdom began to be linked to a new god, a new society and kingdom had to emerge. Making the new god responsible for the future of the kingdom was more convincing than trying to replace *Mwari* directly with something else.

In the Mwenemutapa kingdoms, there were other structures that were looked upon for divine providence. The royal household had three key positions to assist the Mutapa to rule: *Newanji*, *Semukadzi* and *Binga*. This system of rule continued to be observed until the 18th century. The king's sister, *Newanji*, became caretaker-king when the king passed on. The Semukadzi, also the king's sister, performed the role of connecting the Manyika people to their Mwari through the Manyika Ancestral Spirit medium called *Mhondoro*. The extended role of Semukadzi made her not only close counsel to the king, but part of the system of governance. The Semukadzi must have been held in high regard by the people since, as Bhila tells us "it was she who predicted and provided answers to national disasters such as famine, epidemic diseases and wars."[26]

As it was in the Kingdom of Mwenemutapa to the north west, the Kingdom of Manyika had various systems that were used for organisation and governance of the kingdom. The role of rain makers was central to how the king maintained belief not only in himself, but also his rule and the institution of kingship. The *Mwari*, whom the Manyika believe to be their creator, communicated through the king

---

[26] [Bhila, The Manyika and the Portuguese 1575-1863, 1971]

and the rain makers. Belief and worship is essentially bestowed on themselves, or those from their lineage who passed before, with the rain makers and the king acting as a medium to Mwari. Bhila describes a sacred tree, *Muti usine zita*, found in the lands of Mbire, where the royal court and rain makers go to perform ceremonies and offer sacrifices.[27]

Without ascribing a single belief and the same ancestral spirits to all peoples of the Lower Zambezi Valley, the belief in divine figures including *Mwari* has always been central to how the societies functioned and shared a destiny. *Mudzimu*, the Supreme Being around the Sabi region is *Nkulunkulu* in the Thukela and Nkomati region. The name *Somandla* is often used to describe the all encompassing powers of the creator. In Swahili, the word for the a god, *Mwalimu*, was derived from a similar belief and deity closely resembling the Mwari of BaKalanga.

3.3

RAIN MAKING BELIEFS AND POLITICAL POWER

THE great story teller, historian and spiritualist Tata Vusamazulu Credo Mutwa, pointed to the accessible shards of evidence for a world that was once more closely aggregated, before venturing outwards, and will converge once more. Consciousness in the present and what is observed are used as a bond to the world beyond,

---

[27] [Bhila, The Manyika and the Portuguese 1575-1863, 1971]

RAIN MAKING BELIEFS AND POLITICAL POWER

observed Tata Mutwa. Everything from the moon to the sun, and all else in between, have been looked upon as connections to the creator of all things by peoples of all societies. It was not long before natural events like thunder, lightning and rain would be interpreted as messages from beyond. The earliest people to translate the messages, or to claim to understand the messages, became the earliest leaders in the early societies.

Credo Mutwa wonders if the etymology of "rain" tells us something. The sound required to say the word bears, close resemblance in the ancient language of *Abantu*. The Bantu are all peoples of various groups from *Mosi Oa Tunya* falls to *Ukhahlamba* mountains. In IsiZulu rain is *infula*, closely resembling a river where it ends up, *umfula*. In Latin, *pluvius* for rain mirrors *fluvius*.[28]

As early as people have inhabited their lands, they have looked to change their daily lives, whether through hunting, farming, building their houses or deciding to migrate. Unaccommodating weather caused migrations of groups from one area to another. It is unsurprising that people needed guidance in lean times, not only to determine the source of the changes in fortunes they were experiencing, but search for a return to better times. Rain makers probably emerged in this vacuum as the people who could connect to the Supreme Being that can make the rains return.

The time of the earliest rain makers did not begin at Nzimabgwe, Mapela or Matobo. For as long as people can remember, it was believed that Mwari used to visit his people. Mwari's arrival was preceded by the sudden cracking od thunder with a flash of lightning. The arrival could not be missed since it also brought good news. The people would look up the sky and begin ululating, dancing and singing in welcome songs for Mwari.

Nzimabgwe had a centralised the system of rain making

---

[28] [Vusamazulu Credo Mutwa, Indaba, My Children, 1964]

THE KINGDOM AT NZIMABGWE

which was known to members of a clan. The link between those believed to have rain making abilities and their elite place in the society was one of the first indicators of status in the society. The theory goes that the first leaders of clans emerged and rose in rank to be viewed as kings due to their rain making abilities. The king's position and power were derived partly from his claim of being able to perform the role of delivering requests and gratitude to the Supreme Being, *Mwari*. In turn, the citizenry respected and revered rain makers for their access to Mwari, who provided rains, kept the land fertile and delivered providence to the people and their king.

The King in his role as the rain maker relied on rain doctors to perform the rain calling ceremony. Rain makers and healers came to have a close audience with the king creating an interdependent relationship. The ceremony was sacrosanct and steeped in secrecy with only a few insiders participating in the rain making. Zakes Mda captures the role of the king in the novel *The Scultor of Mapungubwe*:

> The King as a living ancestor had performed his role of entreating his fellow ancestors - those who were in the ground - to request Mwali to wet the land so rivers could flow, fields could luxuriate and cattle could fatten ... A strong king was a strong rainmaker.

There is an important link between rain making abilities and the emergence of a broader belief system. The Supreme Being, Mwari for the BaKalanga, was seen as responsible for the abundance in rains the lands enjoyed. Rainmakers were the only earthly beings capable of communicating with the rain gods. Without clarity on which belief emerged first, we can see the role of Mwari throughout BaKalanga cultures and customs which are passed down the generations.

We are naturally led to imagine specific places and sites where worship and offerings were carried out to the Mwari.

What features would be required of the site? What would the offering entail? The practice would not be unique to the early BaKalanga. The Aztec Kingdom from 1100 until the arrival of Cortez in Mexico in 1519, is one reference out of many of peoples developing their own belief system.

There is a well known shrine at Nyamungwe river where the BaKalanga are believed to have worshipped the rain creator *Mwari*. The site is also the burial place of successive BaKalanga kings. The city state that grew nearby came to be known as Nzimabgwe and is understood to be where the belief in Mwari expanded. It is significant that there was one Supreme Being that the clans believed in, unlike the many gods of the Egyptians, leaving aside the failed experiment of Pharaoh Akhenaten who tried to introduce a single sun god, the *Aten*. For BaKalanga, strong evidence points to a single creator, Mwari, who they praise for good fortune and appeal to for divine intervention in times of scarcity, which later develops into an organised belief system seen in pre-war rituals and expanded customs beyond the traditional rain making association.

Matobo Hills is another sacred ground that remains etched in the conciousness of many clans as a centre and a spiritual home of rain making. Matobo retains its history owing to the site's reverence as a place of meeting for past kings and rain makers. Even in present day Zimbabwe, people still travel with *zviyo*, the red millet, and home made beer as offerings to give at Matobo. This practice of offering has survived to modern day ceremonies and festivities. Before the home made brew of *buganu*[29] is enjoyed by those gathered, a small portion is poured into the ground as an offering to ancestors with a rendition of a poem or song.[30] It is quite amazing to see a tradition began be-

---

[29] A home beer made using marula fruit fermented over many months.

[30] Author's personal observation and participation on multiple occasions in South Africa, Swaziland and Mozambique particularly in the presence of grandparents and the elders. The practice is known today as

THE KINGDOM AT NZIMABGWE

fore Nzimabgwe, Mapungubwe or Mapela Hill still being applied in a modern context. The belief in paying respect to those who passed before remains is engrained very deep in the people below the Zambezi Valley.

Rain making ceremonies take place at other sacred sites of historical significance like Domboshava and Matonjeni. King Mzilikazi is buried at Matonjeni, not far from Matobo Hills. He was known to pay respects to the local rain makers and allowed them to settle when he moved into the area. Malaba[31] counters the view that system of worship and offering by rainmakers was fixed in a single "...rock or mountain." The centre of the practice was in the rain makers themselves, irrespective of location. Malaba puts forward the Njelele worship system as one that thrived and spread with new clans that formed mainly because it catered to community and regional problems rather the personal with peace, harmony and unity at the core of the message being shared. The period after the harvest, *Mhawuri* or *Phatwe*, the month of August was followed by various offerings of gratitude and not just requests in lean years or when hardships descended.

Over time, the custom of rain making has taken different forms in various groups. The BaLobedu people were known throughout Southern Africa for their Queen Mudjadji who had rain making powers. Queen Mudjadi was known by kings as far east as the lands ruled by Sgidi kaSenzangakhona, better known as Shaka. He is said to have dispatched a delegation to Queen Modjaji requesting assistance and better rains for his people.

BaPedi people call their rain makers *Moroka*. In each village they are charged with connecting with the spirit medium in times of drought and in times of plenty, to keep the deities and ancestors satisfied. Rain makers know that to wield the power to bring rain belongs to the creator. They

---

Kuphahla.
[31] [Malaba, The Mwali of Njelele and the Story of BaKalanga, 2011]

believe they can connect with the creator, who is in all people, accessed through the spirit medium. The Moroka invoke special ceremonies with animal offering, song, dance and prayers to ancestors to find out the cause of a prolonged drought in one case. Offerings and other celebration ceremonies are performed throughout the seasons to appease the creator.

3.4

BaKalanga: People Of the Sun

NZIMABGWE the World Heritage site, is the centre from which a larger kingdom was ruled. Its famous monuments like the Conical Tower still stand since they were built in the early 14th century. There are competing views stating that the features found at Nzimabgwe had been expressed in a similar form at Mapungubwe or Bambandyanalo. Other views state the the characteristics of the Nzimabgwe were observed earlier at Mapela or Gumanye.

At a later time, beginning around the mid-15th century, a similar culture would thrive at Kame, the capital of Butua Kingdom. To the north of Nzimabgwe, the Kingdom of Mwenemutapa expanded and became the new centre around various kingdoms including Barwe, Birwa, BaTonga, Teve, Danda and Manyika.

Larger groups and smaller clans of people lived and migrated around these kingdoms. The largest known groups are the BaKalanga and BaTonga. In various archive documents, BaKalanga are referred to as *Mocaranga* and BaTonga are called *Mongas* or *Batongis* by JD Santos in Ethiopia Oriental[32]. BaKalanga and BaTonga are present in various locations from the Zambezi valley interior to the coastal areas of the Indian Ocean in all three forms of evidence which we study: documentary archives, archaeological findings and the Traditions. There were many other clans who identified distinctly from the larger groups whilst living in the same kingdom. As familiar in modern times as it was in antiquity, other groups were absorbed into new groups and identities over time.

In his seminal work on the history of BaKalanga, the historian Ndzimu-Unami Moyo introduces us to the clans who to day form distinct groups, but are part of the larger BaKalanga identity. The differentiation continues to expand with the history process itself. This is a continuation of lineages and the formation of new groups, as it was for the early BaKalanga. Societies that started as small groups expanded then seceded, with their economic success dictating the extent of this expansion among other factors. Naturally, societies would attract and absorb other people who assimilated in language, customs and beliefs to some extent. The new people contributed to the culture and practices of the new ruling class and group, consciously or otherwise. The reverse, where a larger group adopts the customs of the smaller and newly arrived people, can also be found in many societies across the world.

In many cases, the new ruling class adopts the culture of the defeated nations. Tea drinking dates to 3rd millennium BCE in China but it was not until 1500 years later that the rest of the world had any. Getting access to tea has resulted in the military battles that took place after the first few sips of tea were tasted in Venice in 1560 CE. Today, some traditions we think of as originating from "The Land of the

---

[32] [Santos, Ethiopia Oriental e Historia do Oriente, 1609]

Rising Sun", have been completely transformed from their Chinese origins. Buddhism, the Samurai code, calligraphy all arrived in a different form in Japan around 607 CE[33].

The formation and growth of the group of people known as BaKalanga, "Of The Sun", was not only in part to new clans joining the larger group but also due to separations. Conflicts would split a group into new identities made up of the former large group. Migration and intermarriage creates new identities and histories of their own. We now turn to the histories of many BaKalanga clans.

Moyo lists the following BaKalanga clans who belong to the same group and identity:[34]

BaKalanga	BaLozwi	BaTwamambo
BaNambiya	BaLemba	BaTembe
BaLobedu	VhaVenda	BaBirwa
BaLembethu	BaTswapong	BaShwangwe

As readers of history will know, the list is not exhaustive. We can add the *Torwa* people who some consider to be of the same lineage as BaLozwi, or the reverse, with BaLozwi assimilating Torwa culture. Both clans certainly occupied the same kingdom as we will see, but we will be led by the evidence before we make generalisations about the Kame based kingdom around 1450 CE. We could add *Korekore* and *Singo* peoples to the list of BaKalanga clans. The Korekore peoples were perhaps recent arrivals in the Lower Zambezi. Their clan name has wrongfully become a pejorative noun for other immigrant groups or outsiders, in a way that is reminiscent of how the Calvinist Protestants group known as the Huguenots, fled religious persecution from France following the 16th century Reformation, and sought *refuge* in other countries giving rise to the word "refugees." A group of Huguenots sailed to South Africa settling in an

---
[33] [Braudel F, A Histoty of Civilisations, 1995]
[34] [NdzimuUnami Moyo, The Rebirth of BuKalanga, 2012]

area renamed the "French Corner", or Franschhoek.

If a BaKalanga group has been left out from the list before, this does not mean there is a conscious effort to exclude. This work is a small part of documenting and discussing history, a process that is always changing, growing and being enriched by more information. The different BaKalanga clans make various appearances in archive documentation and recorded Traditions. BaKalanga are mentioned directly as inhabitants of Mwenemutapa, and we are told of BaLozwi arriving and rising to power in the Butua Kingdom in 1683.

There is no single way to identify a people or their kinship. The TshiVenda saying that "a stranger may prove to be a relative" captures this wisdom. Totems, in addition to the direct bloodline, are the most common emblem used to identify BaKalanga.[35] Totems, *mitupo*, are notable for BaKalanga because they feature animal names. With the passage of time, unique totems can confound and appear distinct when translated or spelled differently. And this is before we take into account the changes in families from marriages or migration.

According to Ndzimu-Unami, BaKalanga are the only people that use animal name totems in the region, with other groups ranging from clan names derived from their kings, areas of settlement, battles or other momentous events in history.[36] Here are some examples of names which are BaKalanga in origin: Sibanda or Shumba (Lion), Nkomo (Cattle), Dube or Tembo (Zebra), Mpala (Antelope), Vundla (Hare), Nyoni (Bird), Nyathi (Buffalo), Mpofu (Eland), Mpunzi (Goat), Ngwenya (Crocodile), Zhowu, Tlou

---

[35] BaKalanga family is derived from parents, brothers and sisters. There is no uncle or aunt but the actual father, big and small fathers. Both patrilineal society (BaTembe) and matrillineal (BaLobedu) structures exist within BaKalanga, with totems used then as the venerated sysmbol and emblem to identify members of the same famiy without extending to sixth cousins or whatever that is, and preventing marriage in the same family.

[36] [NdzimuUnami Moyo, The Rebirth of BuKalanga, 2012]

or Ndlovu (Elephant), Shoko or Ncube (Monkey), Dumani, Baloyi, Khupe, Siziba, Moyo and many more. Likewise, BaLobedu and VhaVenda trace their lineage directly to BaKalanga. Moyo writes:[37]

> To us the Kalanga, the identity of the Lozwi is not something that we can spend time fussing over because we have always known that Lozwi are just one of the clans of BuKalanga. They are just another Kalanga clan like the Whumbe of the Tjibelu totem, the Tswapone of the Dumani totem, the Lubimbi of the Shoko totem, the Mperi of the Khupe totem, the Nhaba of the Zhowu or Ndlovu totem, the Mwanyile and the Mange clans, and many other such.

Today, people with these names can be AmaNdebele, AmaZulu, VaTsonga, BaTswana, MaShona, MoSotho and other clans. They could have nationalities like Zambian, Kenyan, German or Brazilian. The changes in the area of settlement by each group, ascension of new kings with new identities, wars or takeover by other clans over centuries have resulted in people everywhere mixing to the extent that one cannot tell which clan they belonged to simply from the family name. For a clan with a history of migration, annexation or rule of another group, the family name alone offers an incomplete history. Friendly unions between peoples, kings and states are yet to be factored in. As Ndzimu-Unami points out, "Dube can be Mthembu or Tembo," literally Zebra, depending on where one is in Southern Africa. The phonetics of the name evolve, the meaning and origin remain the same.

Pathisa Nyathi posits that it is BaKalanga who translated their names to accommodate the arriving AbaNguni, and later still, the arriving AmaNdebele of King Mzilikazi ka-Mashobane. Whungwe became Nyoni – the translation of *Bird* from TjiKalanga. Assimilation. "Over time there were

---

[37] [NdzimuUnami Moyo, The Rebirth of BuKalanga, 2012], p.89; with an updated version available from www.Bulawayo24.com

THE KINGDOM AT NZIMABGWE

many changes: Ndlovu (Gatsheni) who are Nguni, Ndlovu (Gabula) who are Kalanga, and Ndlovu (Mthombeni) who are Nguni" were all once Zhowu, meaning *Elephant*. Variations of the Elephant name include Tlou and Ndou. Some names go across two or more clans. The very AbaNguni sounding name Ngwenya, *Crocodile*, became Mokoena among the BaSotho.[38] Their origin is BaKalanga.

The observed present day differences and ability to directly trace lineage to BaKalanga for the various groups resides in how they met and formed new groups. A process of uniting people from existing clans in an area is different to uniting with the arrival of new people and leaders. The arrival of AbaNguni after 1800 changed the settlements north of the Limpopo basin, both in the centre (Mzilikazi kaMashobane) and in the east (Manukosi kaZikode, Soshangane), whilst Zwangendaba marched through and headed north past the Zambezi river.

We work backwards tracing the lineage of Bakalanga to the earliest kingdoms in the Lower Zambezi Valley. One of the early accounts we have is from the chronicler Diogo de Alcacova who writes to his king on 20 November 1506. This is recorded in the letter whose long title we abbreviate to *Documentos sobre os Portugueses em Mocambique*, with a full description in the bibliography. Due to the length of the text being more than ten pages, weighed against with its importance, we reproduce the sections relevant to Zambezi plateau in the original language of Portuguese it was written in. The English translation follows so they can be read side-by-side. Our view is that the record provided by the first account letter should be left to each reader to experience directly. We then afford the same scrutiny to the text and corroborated the accounts with other sources including Oral Traditions and archaeological evidence.

---

[38] [Pathisa Nyathi, Zimbabwe's Cultural Heritage, 2005]

Alcacova's letter to his king, available freely from www.archive.org is as follows:[39]

> O regno Senhor em que ha o ouro que vem a Cofala se chama **Ucalanga** e he regno muito grande em que ha muytas villas muito grandes afora muitos lugares outros e a propea Cofala he (terra) deste regno se nam como toda a terra da beyra do mar.
>
> ...E podera Senhor huum homen hyr a huuma cydade que se chama **Zimbany** de Cofala que he grande em que sempre o rei esta 10 ou 12 dias se andar hordenadamente...
>
> ...E em todo o regno de Ucalanga se tira ouro e he nesta maneira cavam a terra e fazem como myna que hiram por ella por baixo da terra huum grande tiro de pedra e vam no tirando por veeas com a terra mesturado com o ouro e apanhado o metem em huuma panella e ferve muito no fogo e despoys que ferve a tiram fora e a poee a esfriar e fria fica a terra e o ouro tudo **ouro fyno**.
>
> **E este rey que agora regna senhor em Ucalanga he filho de Mocomba** rey que foy do dito regno e ha **nome Quesarymgo Menomotapam** que he como dizer fuao porque o nome de rey he Menomotapam e o regno Ucalanga.
>
> Ja Vossa Alteza sabe como **doze or treize anos que ha g(u)erra no regno** domde vinha o ouroa Cofala elle he este o Ucalanga a g(u)erra. Senhor foy nesta maneira no tempo de Mocomba Menomotapam pay deste Quesarimgo Menomotapam tinha huum seu pryvado que era grande senhor em seu regno e que governava todo o regno de desterrar e degolar e de to-

---

[39] [Documentos Sobre os Portugueses em Mocambique/Africa 1497-1840], Vol. I, p.389 – 399

*das outras coussas que queriam como rey que se chamava **Changamir e era justica** moor del rei e o nome deste justica moor he amyr asy como dizemos governador. E este amyr tinha no regno muitas villas e lugaresque lhe o rei tinha dera e estando o amyr em suas terras fazia se grande polo mando que tinha no regno e aquyria muita jente asy. E outros pryvados do rei com enveja comecaram a dizer a el rei que se queria **o amyr alevantar com regno** que o matasse...*

E quando o amyr vyo que el rei asy queria hordenou de o matar na cydade homde estava que se chamava Zunbanhy e levou consygo mutia jente e quando chegou junto com a cydade que souberam os grandes que estavam com el rei que vinha foram no receber e quando o viram vyr daquela maneira nom quyseram estar na cydade e foram se fora e o amyr foy se as causas del rei que eram de pedra e barro muito grandes e todas terreas e entrou homde estava el rei...

*...e como (Changamir) o matou (Mocomba Menomotapam) alevantou se com o regno e se fez rey e lhe obedeceram todos e regnou 4 anos pacyficamente. E ficaram a el rei Mocombo 22 filhos e todos lhos matou o amyr senam huum o mais velho que era ainda moco que ha nome **Quecarymgo que agora he rey** e este fogyram com elle pera outro regno de huum seu tyo e depoys qye foy de 20 anos se veeo apoderar do regno de muita jente da de seu pay...*

*...e ficou do amyr huum seu parente que se chama **Toloa que agora faz a g(u)erra com huum filho que ficou do amyr a el rei Quecarimgo.** E el rei Quecamrimgo mandou ja mutias vezes dizer a Toloa que fosem amigos*

> *e o Toloa nom quer e diz que poys elle matou seu senhor que elle ha de matar a elle **e desta maneira Senhor se alevantou a g(u)erra e esta ainda oje.***
>
> *E asy Senhor trabalhey de saber de que maneira se podiriam fazer pazes antre estes ambos o rei de Ucalanga e o Toloa. Diseram me que se nom podiam fazer senam por el rei de Cofala ou por el rei de Quiloa...*

The snapshots of the ten page letter quoted are part of the ethnographic record from 1506 and a few years before. Alcocova has just arrived and narrates some observations by his predecessor Anhaia. At the time, BaKalanga were under the rule of Mwenemutapa Chikuyo Chisamarengu when the Portuguese arrive, spelled wrongly numerous times as *Quecarimgo*. We learn that his father who previously ruled Bakalanga was Mwenemutapa Nyahuma Mukombero, named as *Mocomba*.

At once, we have six potential polities that the travellers interact with: Mwenemutapa, BaKalanga, Zimbabwe, Torwa, Sofala and Kilwa. We know that the *Mutapas* were leaders of BaKalanga people. Who were the Torwa, said to be in competition and at war with Mwenemutapa? How does Zimbabwe, where the textquotelarge city was based fit in this competition narrative? Or Sofala and Kilwa? The letter attracts different interpretations. As Marina Hyde once asked, and we ask the same of Alcocova, "can one daunting believe this aunt?" What one takes from the tale and removes is left to every reader.

THE KINGDOM AT NZIMABGWE

The translated letter in English corresponding to the Portuguese sections is as follows:[40]

> The kingdom, Sire, whence the gold comes to Sofala is called **Ucalanga** and it is a very great kingdom in which there are many very large towns and many other villages besides, and Sofala itself belongs to this kingdom as does all the land along the shore.
>
> And, Sire, a man may go to a city called **Zimbany** de Sofala, which is big and is where the king always lives, in 10 or 12 days walking at an orderly pace...
>
> ...gold is made over the whole kingdom of Ucalanga and it is done in this manner: they dig into the earth after the fashion of a mine and they go underground for the distance of a stone-shot and as they go, they take from the veins the soil mixed with the gold and gathering it they place it in a pot and boil it well over a fire and after it has boiled, they set it aside and let it cool and once cooled there remains the soil and the gold, **and it is fine gold**...
>
> And this **King, Sire, who now reigns in Ucalanga is the son of Mocomba** who was king in this kingdom and he is **called Quesarymgo Menamotapam** which is like saying king so-and-so, since the word for king is Menamotapam and the kingdom Ucalanga.
>
> Your highness already knows how for **twelve or thirteen years there has been war** in this kingdom whence the gold comes to Sofala; this kingdom is Ucalanga and the war, Sire, was thus. At the time of Mocomba Menamotapam father of Quesarimgo Menamotapam there was a favourite of the king who was a great lord in his kingdom and who ruled the whole kingdom exilling beheading and acting in all things as king, and was called **Changamir and was the king's chief justice** and the word for justice is Amyr. And this Amyr owned many towns and villages in the kingdom given him by the king. And

[40] [Documentos Sobre os Portugueses em Mocambique/Africa 1497-1840], Vol. I, p.389 – 399

within his lands the amyr became great through the power he held in the kingdom and in this way acquired many people, and the other favourites of the king enviously began telling the king the **amyr wished to make himself master of the kingdom** and that he ought to kill him.

And when the amyr saw that the king wished it resolved to kill him in the city where he lived which is called Zunbanhy, and he took with him many people and when he came before the city and the great ones who were with the king knew that he was coming, they went out to receive him but seeing the manner in which he came they would not stay in the city and went away and the amyr went into the houses of the king which were of stone and clay and very large and on one level and entered where the king was...

...and **(Changamir) having killed him (Mocomba Menomotapam) he roused the kingdom and made himself king** and all obeyed him and he reigned peacefully for 4 years and king Mocombo left 22 sons but the amyr killed them all, save one who was the eldest but a youth, whose name is **Quecarymgo and who is now king**, and they fled with this son so another kingdom belonging to an uncle of his, and when he was 20 years old he came to take possession of the kingdom with many of his father's people...

...the **amyr left a kinsman called Toloa who with the remaining son of the amyr now wages war against king Quecarimgo.** And king Quecarimgo sent many times to Toloa offering his friendship but Toloa will not have it saying he killed his lord and he will now kill him. **And in this manner, Sire, was the war started and goes on today.**

And this, Sire, I laboured to find by what manner to make peace between the two kings of Ucalanga and Toloa and I was told that this could not be done save by the king of Sofala or the king of Kilwa.

Scholars have poured every detail in this letter. They

THE KINGDOM AT NZIMABGWE

have analysed the other countless letters published at later dates. The detailed study and analysis provides a caution which should accompany the reading of the letters, or any historical account. History is made and written in the context it occurs in. For example, Zimbabwe appears to be identified as being the same state as the *BaKalanga Kingdom of Mwenemutapa*. The archaeological evidence points to the Mutapas being a new centre of power, presumably as Nzimabgwe was in decline but the state still existed. The word *Nzimabgwe* also means the "House of Stone". These were certainly built by BaKalanga or their descendants and they could be found in any of the kingdom. Great Zimbabwe was the largest and one of the earliest of these. How do the archives compare to the Traditions?

The Oral Traditions collected by DN Beach corroborate the movement of BaKalanga clans from the present day area of Guruhuswa in southwest Zimbabwe to the north.[41] The area they settled in had its centre at Mount Fura. Accounts confirm the contemporaneous rise of Mutapa in the north with similar dry stone building and other cultures that were found in Nzimabgwe earlier. BaKalanga go back to at least 1250 from their recorded capital at Nzimabgwe. Pikirayi notes that the "Karanga expansion northwards during the 15th century must have been triggered by the discovery of more lucrative goldfields in the region that they tried to control..."[42]

Before retracing BaKalanga to the period before Nzimabgwe, let us acknowledge another kingdom referenced in the letter of Alcacova: *Toloa*. The Kingdom of Butua was led by the Torwa, which translates as "foreigners." The Torwa were in a dispute with the Mwenemutapa Kingdom led by Mutapa Chikuyo Chisamarengu (1494 - 1530). This record confirms the third party in the region: Torwa were clearly independent and in competition with Mutapa. We

---

[41] [Beach, Mutapa Dynasty: Documentary & Traditional Evidence, 1976]

[42] [Pikirayi, Great Zimbabwe in Historical Archaeology, 2013]

learned from Pikirayi that the origins of Torwa are unknown but he makes the plausible assumption that some groups were part of Nzimabgwe.[43]

Two other kings are mentioned by Alcocova, the King of Sofala and the King of Kilwa. When this information is combined with maps of the day and recorded Oral Traditions, what can we make of it? For now, it will not be surprising to observe that the BaTonga peoples occupied most of the coastal areas. On 26 June 1516, Almada wrote of "news came to me from the interior by a leading Moor, whom they call Quatyvo, who came from Outonga where gold is found..." Our view is that the BaTonga people did not have a centralised polity. BaTonga were separate small clans under the rule of various local kings, called *Mpfumo*. There was no recognised ruler of a larger kingdom, the king of kings, as BaKalanga clearly had. Interestingly, the KiKongo speaking peoples of modern day Angola and Congo used a similar word, *Mpfumu*, as a title for their kings.[44]

BaKalanga, as both rulers and inhabitants of the Mwenemutapa Kingdom from 1450 to 1800, are firmly woven into all histories of the region. We found that they were one of the people at Nzimabgwe during its height in the period 1250 – 1450. Debate continues to firm up the view that BaKalanga moved between the kingdoms, but Pikirayi's surveys found evidence that the leaders of Mwenemutapa Kingdom had a link to the old Kingdom at Nzimabgwe.[45] What evidence can we present of BaKalanga at Mapungubwe or Gumanye, or even Mapela in the era before Nzimabgwe?

---

[43] [Pikirayi, Great Zimbabwe in Historical Archaeology, 2013]

[44] Correspondence by author with colleague who spoke KiKongo as a native language; not named since we do not have permission yet.

[45] [Pikirayi, Ceramics, Global Networks of Trade and Interaction, 2012]

3.5

THE ROLE OF BEADS, CERAMICS AND POTTERY IN ARCHAEOLOGICAL EVIDENCE

CERAMICS from various archaeological sites contain manufacturing techniques that allow differentiation. Observable patterns, style and geographical location are used for classification. And, there is the material composition and production methods – unobservable to the naked eye – that can be analysed for sources of origin. Combined with recorded history and collected ethnography, ceramics are a central component of understanding the history of the Lower Zambezi Valley.

In a study of ceramics excavated from various sites in Mozambique and Zimbabwe, PJJ Sinclair and his team used the identified patterns to map the likely migration, or at least the transfer of pottery skills, from one community to another over time.[46] The work of Felix Chami on glass beads from Mkukutu in Tanzania, led to the discovery that they were 3rd century Roman beads.[47] The scholarship in this field continues to throw up a few answers with many more questions alongside.

Understanding pottery methods is invaluable to researchers for the evidence they gain about the Early Farm-

---

[46] [Sinclair PJJ et al., Analyses of slag, iron and ceramics..., 1988]

[47] [Chami Felix, Roman beads from the Rufiji Delta, Tanzania, 1999]

ing Communities. We concentrate on the Early Farming Community period beginning in 100 CE, but pottery as old as 30,000 BCE is documented. Not only does the pottery provide an indication of time, style and skill, archaeologists have used evidence from pottery to understand migration and even propose the cultural phase of the community. Findings of 7th century glass beads at Chibuene in Mozambique and from dozens of other locations in Zimbabwe provide evidence of ancient trading links.

When the Early Farming Community sites in the Limpopo basin attracted genuine research, it was the pottery that would expand understanding. The theory put forward by archaeologist Thomas Huffman is challenged by his contemporaries. Professor Huffman studied the pottery styles at Mapungubwe, Great Zimbabwe and Khami. He proposed that the period when a class based society emerged – from the kin based one – could be understood in the context of ceramic styles. But, his peers require more evidence for this leap.[48] Nonetheless, Huffman's findings on elite burials, separated living and the classification he created for ceramic styles has advanced knowledge of the early cultures.

Ceramics and earthenware have a long tradition as a process that captures the history of a people. Because they withstand physical or chemical changes over centuries, they provide a window into their identity and the daily lives of a people expressed directly through the pottery. Culture and ethnographies, however, are not easily projected from the excavations. Consider for a moment excavations on a grand scale. The evidence from the x-ray scan of Tutankhamun's fractured leg, clearly shows that he sustained injuries which led to his death. There were 130 walking sticks in his burial chamber. How the injury occurred and what event led to his death in 1323 BCE continues to attract

---

[48] [Huffman, Mapungubwe & Great Zimbabwe: Origin of, 2009]

THE KINGDOM AT NZIMABGWE

a new theory by the day.

Some of the early ceramics were recovered from a site called Chifumbadze in present day Mozambique. We come to that later. Turn for now to an iron smelting site in Matola which was dated as one of the earliest in Mozambique at 0 - 100 CE. Archaeology stretches the window of evidence much further back. Pottery from Dundo dated to 800 — 900 CE was a continuation of the style found at Matola. Manyikeni, Hola-hola and Chivowa Hill displayed the same pottery style and continuation from 900 – 1700 CE. The various pottery shards dated to different period but maintained the same characteristics. Further afield, the site in Nhachengue, Mozambique was distinct, as was the Chivowa Hill site in Zimbabwe in 1800 - 1900 CE.

Long known traditions of firing clay and making pottery were transferred through generations and evolved over time. The end results were sophisticated techniques that enabled different earthen ware to be made. For example, pottery for carrying water had to permeable to provide the cooling effect whilst pottery for cooking needed to withstand higher temperatures. PJJ Sinclair describes the cooking ware pottery techniques.[49]

> The permeability must not be too great and this was avoided by firing the pottery in a reducing atmosphere...The proper choice of certain raw clays, the ability to manipulate firing conditions in order to obtain the accurate density for a special function, demonstrates a manufacture, based on sophisticated techniques and long traditions.

---

[49] [Sinclair PJJ et al., Analyses of slag, iron and ceramics..., 1988]

3.6

NZIMABGWE BEYOND ITS BORDERS AND NEIGHBOURS

ONE of the earliest reference to "Zunbanhy" from external sources is from the administrative letter by Alcacova in 1506. The letter is followed later by the Fernandes' journey to the court of Mwenemutapa in 1511, with no direct references to Nzimabgwe, except second hand accounts of the "King of Menomotapa and houses of stone." Duarte Barbosa, who travelled as a 14 year old to India, mentions a great town called "Zimbaoche."[50] The most detailed account of Nzimabgwe comes in 1531 from Vincente Pegado who was based at Sofala. Pegado writes:[51]

> Among the gold mines of the inland plains between the Limpopo and Zambezi rivers there is a fortress built of stones of marvellous size, and there appears to be no mortar joining them...This edifice is almost surrounded by hills upon which are others resembling it in the fashioning of stone and the absence of mortar, and one of them is a tower more than 12 fathoms (22 metres) high. The natives of the country call these edifices Symbaoe, which according to their language signifies court."

The letter of Alcacova is peculiar. Keep in mind that that Alcacova's description of Nzimabgwe is from second hand accounts of BaKalanga, BaTonga, Swahili traders and presumably his predecessor Anhaia's reports. Alcacova did not

---

[50] [Duarte Barbossa, Livro de Duarte Barbossa, c.1516]

[51] [Barros, Da Asia: Dos Feitos, Que os Portugueses Fizeram..., 1778], Vol. VI

bear witness to the events he records in detail for posterity. Nevertheless, combining the various administrative documents with recorded traditions and archaeology confirms not only Nzimabgwe and that the kingdom was still viable in 1506, we get narratives of neighbouring kingdoms. The reports emphasize that most of these kingdoms paid tribute to the Mwenemutapa. Whilst each kingdom had a ruler, the Mutapas appear to have been the overlords of the wider Lower Zambezi Valley.

The archives mention another early traveller to the kingdoms neighbouring Great Zimbabwe. This appears to be the closest report which is not from a third party report or hearsay related from one trader to the next towards the coast. The trip to the Zambezi was by a friar, initially travelling to India, who arrived at Sofala on 5 December 1586 and remained for many years. Joao dos Santos discussed his experience in *Ethiopia Oriental*, published in 1622.[52] In chapter XI he writes, *Perto da povoacao de Massapa esta uma mutito alta, e grande serra, que se chama Fura, d'onde se descobre muita parte do reino de Monomotapa*. Santos describes the "ruins," more appropriately remains, of a past civilisation which was based near Mount Fura, which he thinks is the same as *Ophir*. The relevant section of the text translates as follows:[53]

> On the summit of this mountain some fragments of old walls and ancient ruins of stone and mortar are still standing, which clearly shows that once there were house here an strong dwellings...The natives of these lands...assert that they have a tradition from their ancestors that these houses were anciently a factory of Queen of Sheeba...and from this place a great quantity of gold was brought to her, it being conveyed down the rivers of Cuama (Zambezi) to the Indian Ocean...Others say these are the ruins

---

[52] [Santos JD, Ethiopia Oriental e Historia do Oriente, c.1622]

[53] [Santos JD, Ethiopia Oriental e Historia do Oriente, c.1622], p.202

of the factory of (King) Solomon, where he had his factors who produced a great quantity of gold from these lands...not deciding this question, I state that the mountain of Fura or Afura may be the origin of Ophir, whence gold was brought to Jerusalem, by which some credit might be given to the statement that these houses were the factory of Solomon.

Santos is one of the early travellers to create the mythical link of Mutapa gold to the Queen of Sheeba and King Solomon. It was from such accounts that the Kingdom of Mwenemutapa came to be linked to Ophir by the Portuguese and the belief gained followers who tried to locate it. The story was perpetuated over the following centuries and encouraged by the gold trade. It was inevitable that the Bible would be referenced for sources of the tale of King Solomon who ruled around 2000 BCE. The search for more gold mines brought more travellers. Nzimabgwe is about 600 kilometres inland from the nearest point in Sofala on the Indian Ocean. Most of the newly arrived wanted a way to have an audience with the king to get access to the gold trade.

Santos mentions the kings in the Zambezi region of the time: the King of Chicova ruled to the north east of Mwenemutapa; the King of Manyika near Sofala and "King Cambisses" who had just come to power and ruled in the territories below the Zambezi river to the Indian Ocean. Using the list of kings of Mwenemutapa we have compiled from our research, "Cambisses" is actually Mutapa Kapararidze with a reign of 1623 – 1629 CE. Where we could not confirm a Mutapa in the chronology, our list shows a gap, which we are comfortable with. All listed kings have been corroborated across various texts, scholars and oral accounts documented in the bibliography.

3.7

TRADE ON THE COASTAL PORT AT KILWA KISWANI

NZIMABGWE is mentioned frequently in the archives and administrative records of the region with little evidence that it was visited regularly by travellers and traders from beyond the kingdom.

The Moroccan Muslim scholar Ibn Battuta who travelled more of the world than anyone up to that time, sailed to Mombasa, Zanzibar and Kilwa between 1325 - 1332 CE. He reached Kilwa in 1330 and described the port city nearest to the modern day Mozambique border as "one of the finest and most beautiful towns; all of the buildings are made of wood and the houses are roofed with reeds."

The City of Kilwa was an crucial port for the gold trade. Ibn Battuta believed the source of gold lay closer to Inhambane in the south, with other mines found in the interior. In his writing, he made no mention of BaKalanga people or the kingdoms to the south. Word about the Mwenemutapa Kings and the Mansa Musa II of Mali who owned the largest gold reserves, got to the coast at Kilwa and Sofala. Arab traders came and went to the Sofala port trading in the riches in gold.

Vasco da Gama ordered his men to stop at the port city of Kilwa in 12 July 1502. "I sought to meet the king and make peace and friendship with him but he would not meet me," writes a chronicler of the time. One expects the matter would be resolved as peacefully as they had arrived, but "I armed myself with all the men that were with me having

TRADE ON THE COASTAL PORT AT KILWA KISWANI

resolved to destroy him."[54]

Another account from Barros recounts that Mogadishu, Sofala and Kilwa on the coast had been engaged in trade for centuries before his arrival.[55] He writes, "Excited at the prospect of gold trade, the Sultan loaded up a ship with cloth guided by fisherman and sailed to Sofala. He offered the Mwenemutapa gold sellers a better deal and was allowed to erect a Kilwan factory and colony on the island and nudge the Swahili out." The described events set the scene for a scramble for the gold trade, positions and in time, outright control. Bakalanga's trade with the Muslims on the coast was about to be upended.

The merchants at Kilwa did not only trade gold with the Mwenemutapa Kingdom centred at Musapa near Mount Fura in the Zambezi. Ivory, iron, copper and other goods were reaching the coast from the Mwenemutapa Kingdoms in the interior. The Mwenemutapa's middlemen, *Vashambadzi*, in turn imported cloth, jewellery beads and porcelain originating from India, China and Persia. The currency of trade was Kilwa's own minted gold coins. In 1506, 15 *miticals* of ivory were estimated to realise up to 100 in India according to Fogaca.[56] A trade this profitable could only attract more feeders. The kingdoms to the southwest of Kilwa would not be insulated from the approaching demands and ultimately their society. The official currency of Mozambique is known as the *metical* to this day. What was once the *weight* of ivory is now the *measure value* of all goods.

---

[54] [Documentos Sobre os Portugueses em Mocambique/Africa 1497-1840], Vol. I, p.37

[55] [Barros, Da Asia: Dos Feitos, Que os Portugueses Fizeram..., 1778]

[56] [Dickinson, Sofala and the Rivers of Cuama, 1971]

3.8

IVORY ROUTE: SOFALA TO KILWA, THEN MOMBASA, ARABIA AND SOUTHERN ASIA

THE route from Sofala to Kilwa was busy with "sambucos", the shipping vessels of the day. A *sambuk* in Arabic is a vessel sailed with a single small lateen. It could carry 24 men. The sambuk were ideal crafts for sailing along the coast with their versatile latin-rig. A traveller to Mwenemutapa in 1506 wrote [57]:

> In Kilwa there are many sambucos, some as large as fifty ton caravel, others smaller. The big ones are always kept beached until a voyage begins. No nails are used, the hull being stitched with palm fibre which also serves to attach the rudder. They are waterproofed with white resin and gum. The vessels sail from here to Sofala, whence they bring gold, a distance of 255 leagues, and to other places.."

Two types of sailing boats were built and used in Sofala. The seafaring *sambucos* we met, and a smaller one called *bangwas*. Travellers to the region quickly switched to using the locally made vessels to travel along the coast. An idea of the sizes is given by the account of Sobrinho and Homen on their journey to meet the king of Sofala at Pandene, with plans to entrap and kill him.[58]:

---

[57] [Dickinson, Sofala and the Rivers of Cuama, 1971]

[58] [Barros, Da Asia: Dos Feitos, Que os Portugueses Fizeram..., 1778];p.243

IVORY ROUTE: SOFALA, KILWA, MOMBASA AND ASIA

> One day after dark, the eve of the feast of Our Lady of September, the factor set out in two sambuks, one large and another smaller, with twenty-four white men...he went down the river to Pandene where the king was.

From Sofala, local boats were used to travel up the Buzi river which separated the two Kingdoms of Danda to the south, and the Kingdom of Teve to the north. The traders who represented their kings at Sofala port were called *Vashambadzi* or *Mushambadzi* in the singular, written as "mussambazes" in Portuguese administrative records. Vashambadzi were part of the network of trade with the Mwenemutapa Kingdom. The newcomers would covet this network with the view to control the Swahili coastal trading posts, or bazaars, and extend control southwards to Sofala, and eventually to the interior, the heart of Mwenemutapa.

In 1505, the Portuguese sailor Pero d'Anaia and his expedition built the first post of what was to become a fortified trading port at Sofala, at the entrance to the Sofala River in attempt to join the gold trade in the region.[59] Alcacova wrote of the trade between Mwenemutapa Kingdom and the Muslim traders from Kilwa and Mombasa on the coast.[60]

Centuries earlier than the journeys by the Portuguese, in 730 CE, a traveller from present day Morocco famously known as Ibn Battuta[61] would travel to the Mozambique coast. Ibn Battuta travelled from Egypt to Mogadishu, Malindi and Mombasa. He spent one night in Mombasa before heading for Zanzibar and Kilwa Kiswani, "a large city on the coast where the people were black."

---

[59] [Barros, Da Asia: Dos Feitos, Que os Portugueses Fizeram..., 1778]

[60] [Documentos Sobre os Portugueses em Mocambique/Africa 1497-1840], Vol. I, p.389 – 399

[61] Ibn Battuta was named variously as the *The Son of a Duck, Egg-Shaped Bottle*, or better still *Bad Woman with Ellipsoidal Body*.

THE KINGDOM AT NZIMABGWE

He then travelled across the Mozambique Channel to Madagascar before returning to Mombasa, on the Swahili coast as he called it. He was informed about Sofala, "a fornight's journey away" and where they traded gold but did not travel there.[62] Ibn Battuta observed the same locally-made dhows, called *sumbuqs* loaded with various trading goods from bustling activity in the local bazaars. The trade route from Madagascar to port towns on the African coast was well established by 1330 CE.

Ibn Battuta vividly describes the meal he was offered in Madagascar which is probably the first export of the pickled mango recipe:[63]

> He sat the food down and we ate. Their food is rice cooked with ghee, which they put into a large wooden platter, and on top of this they set platters of kushan. This is the seasoning made of chickens, flesh meat, fish and vegetables. They cook unripe bananas in fresh milk and put this in one dish, and in another dish they put curdled milk on which they place pieces of pickled lemon, bunches of pickled pepper steeped in vinegar and salted green ginger and mangoes. These resemble apples, but have a stone; when ripen they are exceedingly sweet and are eaten like other fruit but before ripening they are acid like lemons, and they pickle them in vinegar. When they take a mouthful of rice, they eat some of thise salted and pickled conserves after it.

The long journey from Madagascar back to the Arabian peninsula was assisted by the winds being favourable in the summer monsoon winds of the Indian Ocean. Ibn Battuta observed activities such as pearl diving and Islam was the main faith. Ibn Battuta immediately picked up the change in the diet from rice to millet on the African Coast. He proceeds to taste various fruit which he had not encountered before: banana, coconut and betel. Ibn Batutta is so fas-

---

[62] [Ibn Battuta, The Travels of Ibn Battuta, 2003]

[63] [Hamdun and King, Ibn Battuta in Black Africa, 2005]

cinated with betel leaves that he proceeds to give the full description of how the leaves were turned into a paste to cleanse the breath and for early morning medicinal properties.

We began this journey to trace BaKalanga by focusing on the period around 900 CE. We know about other travellers to Mwenemutapa territories not only from travellers like Ibn Battuta and the Chinese navigator Zheng He, but also from the trade activities recorded in the *Periplus Maris Erythreai*.[64] The Periplus of the Eritrean Sea,[65] written in the 1st or 2nd century AD provides the earliest accounts of trade between Eastern Africa, Arabia and India.

The products traded included ivory, the metals copper, iron, gold and silver, cotton and cloth, tortoise shells, rhinoceros horns, ceramics, glass beads and agricultural goods including cattle, wheat and rice. The southernmost port on the East African coast is named as *Rhapta* in *The Periplus*, from which large quantities of ivory and tortoise shells were exchanged for agricultural tools – hoes, swords and ceramics. Felix Chama notes that the name *Rhapha*, which was the name of the river and the bay according to *The Periplus*, sounds very similar to the river *Rufute* or Lufute which is at the entrance to the present day Kisiju Bay.[66] This name is confirmed in *Da Asia* of JD Barros:[67]

> ...descripcao da terra de Zanguebar... esta comeca em hum dos mais notaveis rios, que da terra de Africa vertem no grande Oceano contra o meio do dia, ao qual Ptholomeu chama Rapto.

What have archaeology, Traditions and archives records taught us about local activity and trading routes? PJJ Sinclair studied the ceramics found in Chibuene, Mozam-

---

[64] [Casson, Periplus Maris Erythreai, 1989]

[65] [The Periplus of the Erythreaan Sea, 1980]

[66] [Chami Felix, The Tanzanian Coast in the First Millenium AD, 1994]

[67] [Barros, Da Asia: Dos Feitos, Que os Portugueses Fizeram..., 1778], Vol II, p.208

bique. Two bowls were found and attributed as Sasanian ceramics. The Sasanid Kingdom was the last Persian dynasty lasting 224 – 651 CE. J. Morais writes of Sinclair's findings:[68]

> The glazed wares from Chibuene include only a single type, namely tin-glazed with splashed painted decoration. This type occurs at sites further north in the coast, at Manda and Kilwa. In addition light blue glazed Sassian Islamic ware occurs at Ponta Dundo 2, and all of these are of possible Persian origin.

The ceramics and glass beads found in various sites from Chibuene – the furthest to the south on the coast – to other sites at Nzimabgwe, Manda and Kilwa, all offer evidence of the coastal trade routes and further links to markets in the interior of the East African coast. The routes date to the 9th and 10th centuries, more than 500 years before the arrival of the Portuguese in 1506. Morais observes "the growing indications of an Indian Ocean trade network which most certainly included the Mozambique coast from late in the first millennium." Further research will add context to these trading links, the people involved but the activity is undeniable. The Portuguese found BaKalanga trading in the region and across the Indian Ocean. Contrary to the view that the Portuguese introduced trade, it was BaKalanga and other peoples of Zambezi Valley who had produced products, created markets and established trade links.

---

[68] [Morais, Early Farming Communties of Southern Mozambique, '88]

4
THE KINGDOM OF MWENEMUTAPA

OF the early kingdoms to emerge from the Lower Zambezi Valley, the Mwenemutapa Kingdom is the most well known outside the region. And by some, within the region. As explored in previous sections, there were many contemporaneously occupied sites with similar homesteads whose inhabitants practised comparable trade craft, art and beliefs.

In the Mwenemutapa Kingdom, some experiences are easily collected from the treasure trove of administrative documents we have. There are many recorded historical events, where the narrative requires scrutiny for it is certainly incomplete and one-sided. But the way events played out is palpable from the record. The Mwenemutapa Kingdom developed and became the most powerful kingdom in the region. On this basis the overwhelming scholarly attention it attracts is understandable, even if, this attention comes with diminished knowledge and enthusiasm for the nearby kingdoms.

THE KINGDOM OF MWENEMUTAPA

There are numerous accounts of negotiations with Kings of Mwenemutapa, who were known as *Mutapas*. The "Mutapa" title started as a name for a specific king. The name was later generalised and became the title of future leaders. A similar process unfolded with Gaius Julius Caesar in 60 BCE Rome. Caesar became the title of *Kaiser* or *Czar* as used by Germany or Russia respectively. The archives present a variety of recorded events too. Records of taxes levied; precise descriptions, weights and prices of traded goods; disputes, fines and banishment from the kingdom, all bring a picture of the year 1500 to life. Momentous times of change and war with travellers to the kingdom are vividly described, although careful interpretation and sometimes suspension of belief is required when reading these texts.

Countless books and articles have been written about the Mwenemutapa Kingdom for other reasons. Increased attention from outside the region in the form of research on past "empires" and nostalgic writing is a different sort of attraction altogether. Some of the travellers to the region took the view of being the first outsiders to arrive in 1506, when incontrovertible evidence exists showing trade with Persia 700 years before that. In the section about trade at Kilwa, we covered the Sasanid ceramic wares from the 7th century AD found in Mozambique.

There is a variety of documentary evidence which shows coastal trade going further back, as early as the 1st millennium AD according to the *Periplus*.[1] Research by multiple scholars including Felix Chami[2] and PJJ Sinclair[3] have shown that artefacts and ceramics recovered from sites at Angoche, Matola and Chibuene date to the 1st millennium AD. We dive into the details of the findings later.

The geographical position of the Mwenemutapa Kingdom close to the Zambezi river provided an outlet to the

---

[1] Periplus Maris Erythraei, written between the 1st and 2nd century AD
[2] [Chami Felix, The Tanzanian Coast in the First Millenium AD, 1994]
[3] [Sinclair PJJ et al., Analyses of slag, iron and ceramics..., 1988]

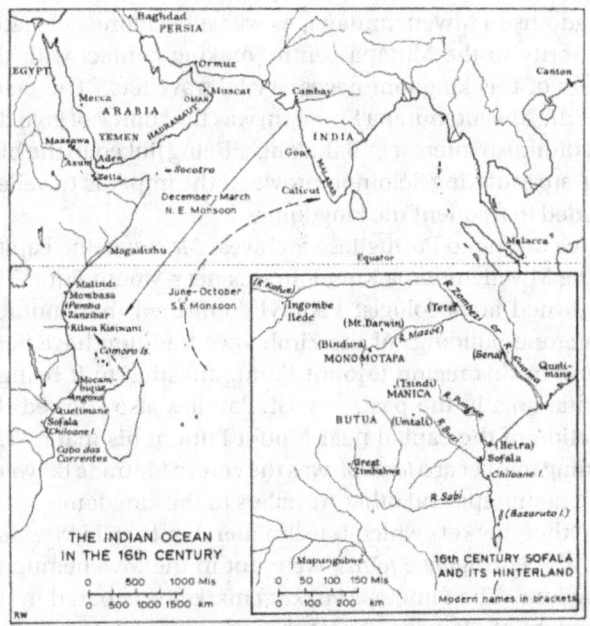

Figure 4.1: The Indian Ocean route to Mutapa states and India. The river Sabi served as a route to Great Zimbabwe in the interior and Butua beyond the Highlands forming the modern border between Mozambique and Zimbabwe. An alternative route was through the river Pungue to the Kingdom of Manyika. The markets at Masekesa, Sena and Tete were reached later through the Zambezi creating competition for the old port as Sofala. The monsoon winds taking ships north in winter was known by the 12th century if not earlier.

Indian Ocean compared to Great Zimbabwe or Butua Kingdom. This made travel and trade links with outside kingdoms far and further afield much easier with Mwenemutapa than Butua in the southern interior. Neighbouring

THE KINGDOM OF MWENEMUTAPA

kingdoms to Mwenemutapa, as we will explore, delegated authority to the Mutapa centre, making contact with the rulers of this kingdom necessary by travellers. The belief that the Mwenemutapa Kingdom was the source of gold did not diminish interest in BaKalanga. Being linked to the biblical story of King Solomon provided the impetus travellers needed to frequent the kingdoms.

According to Portuguese archives, *Massapa*, the capital of the Mwenemutapa Kingdom was near Mount Fura. The renowned archaeologist Pikirayi confirmed that "numerous stone buildings of the Zimbabwe tradition have been found in this region (Mount Fura), attesting to it being a capital area in the past."[4] WGL Randles also showed the location of the capital near Mount Fura in his map.[5] The trading market at *Massapa* was the centre for trade between Mwenemutapa and other travellers to the kingdom.

Other markets which Muslim merchants called *bazaars* and the Portuguese *feiras*, were not in the Mwenemutapa Kingdom. The famous *Masekesa* market was based in the Kingdom of Manyika. Another market was based near Sofala on the Indian Ocean coast, which was part of the Kingdom of Danda. There was clearly a network of trade between different kingdoms in the Zambezi. Exporting to Asia and Arabia on the Indian ocean extended the trade routes.

All forms of interest that the Mwenemutapa Kingdom experienced from the 16th century has resulted in a large volume of writings about the kingdom. Most of the narratives are now being weighed against histories of other kingdoms in the region – Manyika, Danda, Teve and so on. We challenge aspects of the volumes of writings, especially those which do not evaluate the context in which history was made. We shine light on historical narratives that have become popular without a basis in evidence. We offer an alternative narrative where our research yields evidence

---

[4] [Pikirayi, Ceramics, Global Networks of Trade and Interaction, 2012]

[5] [Randles, L'empire du Monomotapa du XV au XIX siecle, 1975]

from sources which were previously ignored. We view past events, in the context they occurred with a fresh perspective.

In the account of the Mwenemutapa Kingdom, we present the evidence in other forms including archaeological findings and the Oral Tradition of other kingdoms nearby. This is not to diminish the achievements of the *Imperio del Monomotapa* as the Portuguese described it. The Mwenemutapa Kingdom was clearly the centre exercising power and dominance by extracting tribute from surrounding kingdoms long after the decline of Nzimabgwe. The building remains and artefacts recovered from what was once a great state at Great Zimbabwe, are there to be observed directly to day. Detailed research enriches understanding and contributes to the picture that emerges. Recording, re-writing and analysing past events creates the space for debate by stating the history of the region in a context closest to the evidence found.

The previously dominating view from archaeologists and historians was that the decline of Nzimabgwe coincided with the rise of a new power in the north east: the Mwenemutapa Kingdom.[6] The Mutapa state survived various challenges, natural catastrophes and internal succession disputes. External challenges that the kingdom oversaw included newly arrived people and travellers to the region including the Rozvi and the Portuguese. We meet the inhabitants of this kingdom and delve into what can be recovered of their lives.

The Mwenemutapata kings ruled not only their kingdom but appear to have exercised suzerainty over neighbouring kingdoms. We know this from the payment of tribute they expected and received from the new and surrounding kingdoms to its territory. The royal families of the new kingdoms were related to the central Mwenemu-

---

[6] [Chirikure and Pikirayi, Debating Great Zimbabwe, 2011]

tapa Kingdom, but increasingly ruled independently. We explore the dynamics of these relationships and how the Mwenemutapa states evolved.

The Traditions narrate the Karanga clans moving from Nzimabgwe to a region called Guruhuswa.[7] The landscape of Guruhuswa is described as a large grassland where the grass is taller than observed elsewhere. This area has been identified to be present day Zimbabwean Highlands to the east by the renowned historian on ancient Zimbabwe: DN Beach. We have no direct evidence pointing to the abandonment of one territory followed by a migration to another. But, we can associate the rise of a nearby state partly, and very loosely, to being influenced by its neighbours. The nature of this influence is unknown and we speculate no further. This is the current view of development for Nzimabgwe and Mwenemutapata: separately, but not entirely unrelated. This is different to saying the residents of Nzimabgwe moved to Mwenemutapa.

Further evidence of separate communities developing their own culture is provided by the research focusing on archaeology in addition to documents and oral accounts. Archaeologists Chirikure and Pikirayi show that the various early settlements in the Lower Zambezi Valley developed independently over time. The belief that the early settlers moved to other sites cannot be attributed to a linear process where a single group and their descendants move from one site to the next. The specific example of Bambandyanalo people, from the area also called the K2 Settlement by researchers who struggle with name Bambandyanalo, is instructive. Chirikure and his team show that the Bambandyanalo people who moved to Mapungubwe (1220 – 1290 CE), whose culture was later expressed at Nzimabgwe (1250 – 1450 CE) is too ambitious following fieldwork at Mapela Hill. Chirikure's team find that the

---

[7] [Beach, Mutapa Dynasty: Documentary & Traditional Evidence, 1976]

4.1

DECLINE OF NZIMABGWE IN 1450 CE, THE RISE OF TWO NEW KINGDOMS: BUTUA AND MWENEMUTAPA

HISTORICAL records and oral accounts are constantly challenged and debated. There is no such debate among historians and archaeologists regarding the last days of settlement at the royal court in the Kingdom of Nzimabgwe. Did the residents gather most belongings and leave? Every artefact found at the site dates to the same upper bound of its lifespan: circa 1450. There was no conflict, war of conquest or takeover by other people. Nzimabgwe was neither sacked nor burnt down. What then made the kingdom fall out of favour, began its abandonment and decline, and which new kingdoms were in favour before the end of 1500 CE?

The most coherent explanation which has been put forward for the departure, for which a consensus exists, appears to be a drought which caused crops to fail for a few seasons. The shortage of water for the livestock and lack of grazing pastures exacerbated the move away from Nzimabgwe, argues one camp. Apparently, the very factor that made the site attractive – the ecological attractiveness of the territory – was what seemed to contribute to its demise. David Beach supports the camp holding this view: the decline of Great Zimbabwe was caused by the pressure on the local environment which became too large to bear.[8]

Having been estimated to have one of the largest populations in the region, perhaps the sizes of both human and animal populations could not support both, especially if there were increasingly failing rains. It would not be surprising if climate researchers were to conclude that climate change of the region around this time was a factor. Research in this area continues to provide insights. Was there a need for resources from further afield that could not be brought to Nzimabgwe? The migration from Nzimabgwe to Mwenemutapa rests on the view that there was a natural migration away from Nzimabgwe caused by the various factors. The only corroborating evidence we find, is that the Traditions point to a drought roughly every five years in the region. This is clearly not enough.

Researchers have advanced other reasons including a decline in gold yields, or over-farming and overgrazing from the huge herd of cattle.[9] A singular narrative is yet to be put forward with decisive evidence to back it. The only clarity from the dating of artefacts excavated is that the end was around the same time – 1450. Perhaps the various changes in the region all contributed, to be consistent with our negation of a single factor or simple story narrative.

In the valley beyond the source of the Gwai river, near Bulawayo, a city grew which the inhabitants called Kame, corrupted to "Khami" in modern day literature and maps. We need not wonder too far to find the reasons why Kame was a preferred location as the centre for a new kingdom. The area has a large concentration of gold resources with some of the best grazing lands below the Zambezi.

---

[8] [Beach, Mutapa Dynasty: Documentary & Traditional Evidence, 1976]
[9] [Ndoro, Great Zimbabwe, 2005]

NZIMABGWE DECLINES, MUTAPA RISES 1450

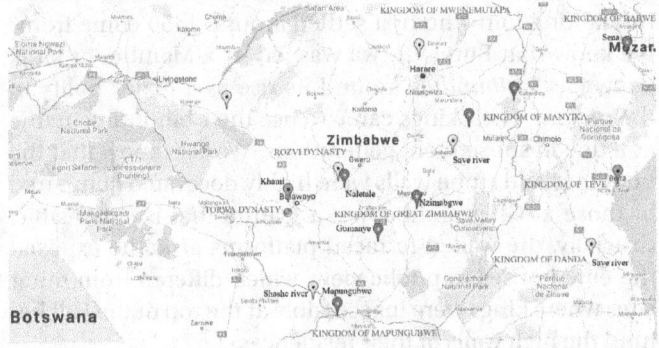

Figure 4.2: The map shows the various chiefdoms and kingdoms between the Zambezi river and the Limpopo river. The shown polities are covered and corroborated by both administrative archive documents, research by archaeologists and collected ethnography grouped broadly as Traditions by clans of the regions.

Kame was the initial capital of the Kingdom of Butua and it thrived until the war of 1644 changed that with inhabitants and the capital moving to Danangombe.[10] Beginning in the 1970s, research by a new group of archaeologists including Thomas Huffman, believed that Kame emerged from the cultures expressed earlier at Great Zimbabwe (1290 – 1450 CE), and before that, those expressed at Mapungubwe (1220 – 1290 CE).[11] Modern archaeologists have challenged this view while the archaeology and Traditions increasingly fail to support it. We dig into the various positions on emergence of Kame next.

The Butua State (1450 – 1683) or Torwa State as it is often called, has been continuously inhabited by different groups and led by different elites. Where did the inhabitants of the

---

[10] [Machiridza, Landscapes & Ethnicity: Hist. Archaeology of Khami, 2020]
[11] [Huffman, Mapungubwe & Great Zimbabwe: Origin of, 2009]

THE KINGDOM OF MWENEMUTAPA

Butua Kingdom who first settled around 1450 come from? We know that Butua-Torwa was led by a Mambo, or king, known as *Chibundule* around its rise as a major polity in the region. Their kings came to use the Chibundule name as a title in subsequent generations. We also know that the buildings and stone walls were highly decorated compared to those at Great Zimbabwe, a feature that is still visible. Crucially, the walled terraced platforms at Kame exposed the elite houses to public view, which differed from other sites where kings were inaccessible at the top of the Hill behind the high walls of their residences.

The first – not earliest – inhabitants of Butua we know were Balilima, a clan of BaKalanga. The chronology showing Kame was occupied earlier than 1450 has already challenged the view that residents of Kame arrived from Great Zimbabwe. The decline of Nzimabgwe did not lead to the rise of Butua, they existed concurrently. Dr. Van Waarden proposes the opposite, offering that Kame could have led to a hastened decline of Nzimabgwe.[12] Features of the society at Kame that are allow comparison of the kingdoms, are distinct and appear independent to be linked directly to Nzimabgwe. Elite buildings were more prominently displayed at Kame with elaborate decorations. The pottery design was more complex with "bands and panels of red ochre and graphite" unlike the homogeneous cross hatched markings for Great Zimbabwe pottery.[13]

The groups found in the Butua Kingdom included BaKalanga, Korekore, Zezuru, VaNdau, BaNambiya and VhaVenda. BaNambiya and VhaVenda clans grew their new identity whilst recognising their BaKalanga forefathers and roots. BaNambiya left Butua when their leader, Sawanga – or Hwange which is now the name of the area of their origins – seceded with a desire to form a new state separate

---

[12] [Van Waarden, The Origin of Zimbabwe Tradition Walling, 2011]

[13] [Chirikure, Manyanga, Pikirayi, Pathways of Sociopolitial Complexity, '13]

NZIMABGWE DECLINES, MUTAPA RISES 1450

from the Rozvi-led Butua Kingdom.[14] The Oral Tradition informs that, at some point in their history, BaNambiya interacted with and mixed their identity with BaTonga. It was normal that as the groups grew and migrated, they came into view of other clans. The concept of one group taking up leadership of another completely different clan before assimilating to the norms of commoners from the defeated group was not unusual. What sometimes appears as a single group of people, reflects deeper and complex interactions. The task for historians attempting to unravel the origin of a people or a cultural feature becomes intractable. We cannot fully rely on language either, as some historians tend to. The Torwa leaders for example spoke TjiKalanga, the language of the people they came to rule at Butua.

Other people in the Kingdom of Butua had arrived from north eastern Botswana.[15] The old theories about the revival at Kame benefiting from the decline of Nzimabgwe simply do not stand any more. Yes there are similarities in the use of dry stone walling and the selection of hill fort landscapes with leaders at the top of the hill. The research at various sites including Kame, Danangombe, Naletale and Zinjanja has provided ample evidence of different pottery styles, a more decorated and visible stone wall building. The timelines indicate that both kingdoms existed contemporaneously.

Research by scholars inspired by David Beach has shone a bright light on the history of the Zimbabwean plateau. The new generation of scholars have expanded on Beach's initial work in Zimbabwe. The archaeologist Pikirayi and his colleagues have examined other sites with remains of Early Farming Community life. Only a selected few sites had received the lion's share of the research attention until the new generation of archaeologist dedicated themselves to the region. Interestingly, excavations at other sites like

---

[14] [Pathisa Nyathi, Zimbabwe's Cultural Heritage, 2005]

[15] [Tlou and Campbell, History of Botswana, 1984]

THE KINGDOM OF MWENEMUTAPA

Mapela Hill and Domboshava add to the knowledge we have about Mapungubwe, Nzimabgwe and Kame, the darlings of the field. As in most fields of scientific enquiry, new information should either confirm what is known, or lead to a revision of what was previously known. The work of the new generation of archaeologists is to be commended as they build knowledge and discard theories without fitting evidence.

The next significant date at Kame was the arrival of the people known as BaRozwi in 1683. As their name translates, "the destroyers," their arrival spelled the end of leadership by the Torwa dynasty at Butua. Over time, BaRozwi would speak TjiKalanga and build a new identity – or retain it – as BaRozwi or BaLozwi with BaKalanga ancestry and lineage. The decline of Nzimabgwe to the east, new leadership at Kame, the growing Mutapa kingdom the north ushered in a changed landscape. The Kingdom of Mwenemutapa would come to exercise suzerainty over all other kingdoms below the Zambezi except Butua under BaRozwi.

In the next instalment of this series, we show that the support of BaRozwi was essential to *Mutapa Nyamaende Mpande*, also known by his baptism name of "Dom Pedro" success in expelling the Portuguese from his kingdom in 1693 with victory at Dambarare. BaRozwi were led by *Changamire Dombo* "who is attested in the Portuguese accounts and who is apparently to be identified with the orally remembered figure of *Mambo Dlembewu*."[16] We found that the letter of Alcocova confirms these events.[17] An extract of the letter is included in the chapter on Nzimabgwe.

---
[16] [NdzimuUnami Moyo, The Rebirth of BuKalanga, 2012], p.90

[17] [Alcacova, Carta de Diogo de Alcacova para el-Rei CC, 1506]

4.2

MWENEMUTAPA KINGDOM AND BAKALANGA

ONE group of peoples who moved from settlement to settlement in the Zambezi Valley, for as long as history is recorded, were BaKalanga. They settled near the arid Kalahari to the west, crossed the Vhembe river to the vast central plains, and others scaled the eastern highlands of Gorongosa towards the coast. Pottery, burial sites and building remains are some of materials we study to learn the history of BaKalanga. Although we give the people of the time a single name, there were a variety of groups and clans.

In the north, BaTonga were the largest population group. Among the many groups in the region at this time, BaKalanga and BaTonga appear to have formed the largest identities. Some of the earliest groups we can locate with certainty are BaKalanga, BaTonga and BaSarwa, if we take the most distinct groups. We know about BaLozwi, at least later but we know they were essentially part of the large BaKalanga group, a clan if you will.

We know that by 1450, the Mwenemutapa kingdom had grown into the organised polity that would exercise its power in the region. When the state was formed is unknown. Mwenemutapa remained intact in various forms – from a centralised state ruled from Masapa, to the increased decentralisation that would see Manyika, Danda and Butua as competitors – until mid 19th century. By some accounts, the Mwenemutapa Kingdom was founded when

THE KINGDOM OF MWENEMUTAPA

Great Zimbabwe was still flourishing, circa 1350. The suggestions from Alcacova is that people from Great Zimbabwe moved on to found another state, the Mwenemutapa kingdom.[18] In time, other dependent provinces and eventually kingdoms would emerge.

Each group had a leader, which is equivalent to an *Induna*, which translated as "Chief". The Induna's people usually carried the same name as that of the leader. This introduces confusion in the historical record at times when leaders change. The classic example is BakaZulu who were a small subgroup of BakaNdwandwe but went on take over various smaller groups in the Thukela and Phongolo in 1800. The name Zulu is better known compared to those that preceded it.

The rulers of Kalanga were known as the *Mambo* but were addressed as the *Mutapa* in the same manner there is a King but he is addressed as Your Highness. Visitors to Kalanga would ask who the leader was to which the local replied: "Nhu Unotapa", meaning "He Who Takes All." The citizens reflected the all-powerful and dominating ruler who governed lands, taxes and metered out punishment for law breakers. The word *Monomotapa* is actually two separate words: "munhu" and "tapa", which together translate as the King or Leader or even Person, who Owns, Conquers or Takes All. The who lived in Kalanga saw the ruler effectively as a "God," who could communicate with *Mwari* to request rains and other blessings.

Having succeeded in navigating through the Cape of Torments, the travellers who met the people of Mwenemutapa recorded the king as "the Monomotapa." They wrote of his "Mocaranga" later described as his "Monomotapa Kingdom." On their arrival, they found the BaKalanga as the largest group, who were the inhabitants of the Kingdom of Mwenemutapa. There were many other groups whom we

---

[18] [Newitt, A History of Mozambique, 1995], p.38

will discuss. We make a clear distinction of what archives recorded at single point in time, which reflects the facts but also understanding and location of the visitor. This could vary significantly from the situation on the ground. After all, the kingdoms covered an area of much larger size that they were used to.

We know the *Mambo* of BaKalanga who united the various clans and groups to be Mutapa Nyahuma Mokombero. He certainly was not the first leader of BaKalanga. He is the Mambo known to us through the historical record and Oral Traditions.[19] Nyahuma Mukombero, called *Mocomba* in the records, reigned in the period c. 1480 – 1490 CE.[20] The history of the Mambos and their rule over the centuries could not have had a wider reach. The dawn of another eventful period in their history was on the horizon.

The rule of Nyahuma Mukombero was followed by a king who came to be known as *Changamire the Usurper*. Changamire's reign was a short 4 years until Nyahuma Mukombero's son, Chikuyo Chisamarengu ascended in 1494. Chikuyo is the first Mutapa to be visited by the newly arrived travellers from Portugal, as documented by Antonio Fernandes in his second trip of 1511–1512 to Sofala and Manyika. Fernandes's first visit was in 1505, but we do not believe he had audience with the Mutapa on that occasion. Fernandes wrote: "the Karanga Chief mines a great deal of gold, baskets of bars and nuggets,... he lives in a great fortress." Reporting on his journey and the state of politics he found, Fernandes went "into the Kingdom of the Changamire who the Mutapa Chikuyo was at war with." Another chronicler wrote of the same king. Alcacova said of Mutapa Chikuyo Chisamarengu: "...rei do Ucalanga era Quecarymgo Menomotapam, filho de Mocomba." Chikuyo Chisamarengu is the king, the son of Nyahuma Mukombero, with Chisamarengu wrongly

---

[19] [NdzimuUnami Moyo, The Rebirth of BuKalanga, 2012]
[20] [Alpers, Dynasties of the Mutapa-Rozwi Complex, 1970]

THE KINGDOM OF MWENEMUTAPA

spelled as *Quecarymgo*.[21]

Mutapa Chikuyo Chisamarengu appears to have opened trade negotiations much earlier. We are told by Figueroa that in February 1506, "the Monomotapa sent a trade mission to the newcomers, demonstrating his willingness to divert trade in gold." A competition had appeared between the Muslim traders on the coast and the newly arrived Portuguese on the scene. The system of administration in the Mwenemutapa Kingdom, one we know well from Oral Traditions, is described by one Portuguese traveller, Bocarro, wrote in 1609:[22]

> *"O Monomotapa tinha mais de 300 leguas de circuito e era dividido em vastos reinos administrados por poderosos regulos, em tor-no dos quais gravitavam certos senhorios chamados encoses."*

Bocarro's evidence that the King who ruled lands of more than 300 leagues[23] in size provides an idea of how well known he was, and the high regard that the Mutapa held in the region. Not only does the *Monomotapa* rule the large territory, but he rules over other "local kings" or provincial governors, called *Inkosi*. Bocarro's account is corroborated by the chronicler of his times, Barros, who wrote about the "the immense territory and riches of the Emperor of Monomotapa."[24]

---

[21] [Documentos Sobre os Portugueses em Mocambique/Africa 1497-1840]
[22] [Bocarro, Decada 13a. da Historia da India, 1876]
[23] A league is an ancient measure of the distance a person can walk in an hour. If one walks 10km in an hour, the estimate given is for 3,000km.
[24] [Barros, Da Asia: Dos Feitos, Que os Portugueses Fizeram..., 1778]

4.3

THE EARLY MWENEMUTAPA DYNASTY: MUTAPAS MUKEMBERO, CHANGAMIRE AND CHISAMARENGU

MUTAPA Nyahuma Mukembero ruled from 1480 to 1490. His rule had ushered in a period of stability, growth and expanding trade, confirmed by the Portuguese when they arrived. Mukembero continued to take tribute from neighbouring states indicating the position of power of the BaKalanga Kingdom of Mwenemutapa.

The focus on the 17th century Mwenemutapa rulers will reveal how Bakalanga clan names have been passed down the generations. The administrative archives of the later period, the 17th century, are discussed in the next instalment of this series. Suffice to state for now that the Mutapa's family totem is *Moyo*, the Heart. Every clan in the BaKalanga Kingdom is known by its totem which identifies the lineage of a people, and is used to pass history from generation to generation. The Moyo family name is one of the most prevalent in Zimbabwe, central Mozambique and northern South Africa today. *Chimoio* remains the name of the area to the west of the Gorongosa mountains, and the central province of Mozambique, bounded by the Sofala province to the east. Chimoio was BaKalanga country in the Mwenemutapa kingdom. The name lives on with places like *Bagamoyo*, "Of the Moyo", derived from the clan's totem name. The historian Ferreira has observes:[25]

> *Cerca de 1490 um dignatario conhecido por Changamire, possivelmente do Totem Moio, chacinou o Mutapa reinante e vinte e dois dos seus filhos. So quatro anos depois, un dos raros sobreviventes, Cacuio Comunhaca, conseguiu controlar de nove a provincia, despois de executar o revoltoso.*

The administrative archives are rich with encounters and testimonies of Mutapa Nyahuma Mukembero. Pacheco refers to him as *Mucombue* whilst Alcacova writes about *Mocomba* with the slightly different dates of reign 1485 – 1494 CE.[26] Both are clearly referring to the same king. Reconciling the sources we have leads us to conclude that Mutapa Mukembero was killed around 1490, so he could not have been king until 1494. Indeed, Alcocova himself informs us elsewhere of a royal family member who challenged the king for the throne. Changamire I, ruled briefly from 1490 – 1494 CE. This sequence of events shows the importance of corroborating various sources, but the researcher still has to set out the chronological framework to tell the history of Mutapas.

The death of Mutapa Nyahuma Mukembero was followed by a battle for succession. *Changamire the Usurper* killed the reigning Mutapa and his children who would have challenged the throne. One of Nyahuma Mukombero's children, Chikuyo Chisamarengu, survived. Four years he regain the throne after challenging and killing usurper. This was a tumultuous period in the Kingdom of Mwenemutapa. It is at this time that the Portuguese arrive. As Newitt notes, "Portugese expansion was a direct product of Portugal's poverty not its wealth."[27] The increase in

---

[25] [Rita-Ferreira, Fixacao Port. e Historia Pre-Colonial de Mocambique, '82]

[26] [Pacheco, Viagem de Tete ao Zumbo; Boletim de Mocambique, 1883]

[27] [Newitt, A History of Mozambique, 1995], p.14

THE EARLY MWENEMUTAPA DYNASTY

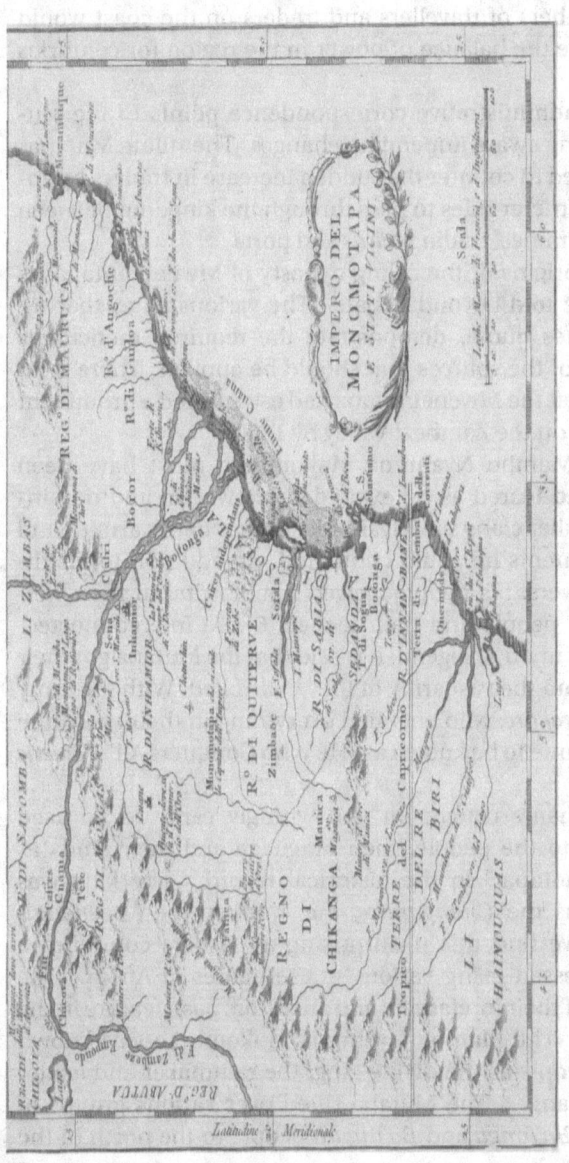

Figure 4.3: Impero del Monomotapa e Stati Vicini 1781. Mwenemutapa and Neighbouring States. Kingdoms of Quiteve, Abutua, Sedanda, and centres at Zimbaoe and Botonga are shown. Zoom into the publicly available map at https://purl.stanford.edu/fp258xw6265 to see trading centres at Massapa, Sena, Tete. Usual language warnings apply.

the numbers of travellers and traders on the coast would challenge the balance of power in the region for centuries to come.

The administrative correspondence points to the Mutapa being aware impending changes. The ruling Mutapas attempted to counter the sudden increase in traders by enforcing stricter rules to pass through the kingdom between the gold mines, trading *feiras* and ports.

The origins of the ruling dynasty of Mwenemutapas is yet to be told beyond debate. The various dates that we sometimes quote, demonstrate the required meticulous reading of the sources that should be applied. There is no doubt that the Mwenemutapa had established a prominent position on the Zambezi Valley by 1450.

The Mambo Nyahuma Mukombero must have been loved and feared as he expanded his wealth and dominion. Smaller clans saw Nyahuma Mukombero's armies and the regiments he could command. In addition to his divine powers, his people viewed him as vital to their welfare, the people and their leaders 6were interconnected. Whether myth or legend, it is said that the Mutapa got their name from the vast army of they controlled. With the army of *Makorekore*, who engulfed everything in their wake, the leader came to be known as "He Who Conquers All", *Mwene Mutapa*.

The name caught on and wrongly came to be used to refer to the people, their language and their lands as "Monomotapa." in the historical record. The king was known as the *Changamire*, the *Mambo*, the *Mwenemutapa*. We find this unsurprising as leaders continue to be addressed using various praise names in Africa. The names of their forefathers and ancestors past, feature in the present. The Mambo Nyahuma Mukombero was known to his people as the divine king, the rainmaker and leader of BaKalanga. The Mutapa ruled over various groups of people: *BaTonga* and *BaTavara* people to the north in the

THE EARLY MWENEMUTAPA DYNASTY

Zambezi valley, *BaKalanga*, *BaNyayi*, *BaNambiya*, *BaLozwi* and *BaTembe* in the central valley beyond the Mbinga and Gorongosa mountains, and many other groups. In the archives, we hear more about a few people with the unintended omission of other clans in the Mwenemutapa polity.

Newitt restates the details of Alcacova's account about the conflict between Changamire of the Butua Kingdom to the west, and Mwenemutapa Nyahuma Mukombero.[28] The events preceded the movement of Mukembero to a new capital in the north:

> "About thirteen years earlier (1494), conflict broke out between the Kalanga ruler Mucombo (Nyahuma Mukombero) and one of his subordinates who carried the relatively common chiefly title of Changamire, but whose clan name was Toloa (as in Torwa or Togwa). In the conflict which followed, Mucombo, the Mwenemutapa, was expelled from his stone-built capital and took refuge with a kinsman."

The internal succession battles were not uncommon in the ruling dynasty. Challenges from provincial governors or semi-independent kingdoms would also grow. By 1512, the challenge from the Kingdom of Butua, led by the Torwa is apparent to Mwenemutapas. King Nyamunda of the southern Kingdom of Danda on the Sabi river begins to exercise disapproval from the Mutapa central rule. Events are about to take another historic turn.

---

[28] [Newitt, A History of Mozambique, 1995]

4.4

DISTINCT AND INTERTWINED BaTONGA AND BaKALANGA PEOPLES IN THE KINGDOMS

THERE are as many views about the people of the Mwenemutapa Kingdom as there were people. The same clans turn up in different kingdoms, as majorities and sometimes as minorities. Were some of the leaders, known as Mutapas, from the same lineage as the people who built Great Zimbabwe? Were they BaKalanga or from some of the clans from the southwest interior? Or did a new kingdom grow to exercise power in the region after local BaTonga came under a paramount ruler who united them? There were various kingdoms by 1500 CE surrounding the Mwenemutapa Kingdom including Barwe, Birwa, Teve, Danda and Manyika.

In searching for answers, the researcher has to appreciate complexity of the subject being studied. From birth place, migration and other political changes which can cause the same people to be found in three territories over time. The case of the people called *Dombe* is instructive. We want to understand the BaTonga, BaKalanga and the other groups. The accounts is told by George Ndlovu to the renowned Zimbabwean writer and historian Pathisa Nyathi.[29]

---

[29] [Pathisa Nyathi, Zimbabwe's Cultural Heritage, 2005]

Ndlovu recounts that the region of Hwange in present day Zimbabwe is dominated by BaNambiya people, which had not always been the case. The area had been occupied by Dombe in greater numbers before the arrival of BaNambiya. Straight away we observe that BaNambiya are well documented as part of BaKalanga. They are a BaKalanga clan. Ndlovu proceeds[30]:

> The Dombe, or more appropriately the Leya, are a Tonga people. They speak a dialect of Tonga. They came from across the Zambezi River to settle in what is now Hwange District....identifies three clans of Mapeta, Chenya and Ndlozi

Many groups of people were settled in the Lower Zambezi Valley by 1500. *BaKalanga, BaRozwi, BaTonga, BaGwambe, BaMaravi, BaSarwa, VaMakua, VaMaconde, VaNwanati, VaHlengwe*, to name a few. We are aided in the distinction between BaTonga and BaKalanga by the varied ethnography and locations where they are found, but this is by no means definite. BaTonga generally occupy the coastal areas, and are increasingly pushed in that direction until the 19th century. This view will suffer the shortcomings of many rules.

In archives that are infinitely useful but equally as challenging to interpret due to the language and questionable veracity at times, we can build a picture from the shards and snippets of information over the centuries.[31] We get

---

[30] [Pathisa Nyathi, Zimbabwe's Cultural Heritage, 2005]

[31] There are many tales in the first hand accounts which leave the reader in doubt. Pero d'Anhaia enters Sofala, marches to see the king, enters uninvited and fights off all the Sofala King's knights before *the king, in great anger* defended himself, which then gives Anhaia the reason to "gave him many wounds until they left him without his kindom and hs life". After celebrating a notable victory, "Pedro d'Anhaia returned to his fotress, being mortal, ...he fell sick of the fevers" and died.[Documentos Sobre os Portugueses em Mocambique/Africa 1497-1840], Vol. III, p.608; One of the best critiques of first hand sources we have seen is from [Naidu, Three Tales of Theal: Biography, History and Ethnography, 2012]

THE KINGDOM OF MWENEMUTAPA

some evidence of the distinction between the kingdoms of BaTonga or smaller polities commonly known as "Chieftaincies", and the larger and centralised BaKalanga kingdoms. Our task is not made easier by trades in common between BaTonga and BaKalanga including alluvial gold mining, trading in metals, ivory hunting, cotton growing and keeping of cattle. Smaller clans specialised in a single trade but there was not enough differentiation at the larger group level or between kingdoms. BaKalanga's identity was tied to the cattle keeping and they had very large herds, whereas the BaSarwa who moved freely kept very few if any.

More misleading to the identity of BaTonga and BaKalanga in the 16th century is the idea that a single name can account for the group identity. BaTonga were made up of numerous clans from the Zambezi to the Sabi and as far south as present day Inhambane. *VaChopi, VaMacuacua, VaNdau and VaMaconde* probably did not see themselves as BaTonga, unlike *BaTsonga, BaRonga, VaBila, VaHlengwe, VaNwalungu or Van'wanati* who view their heritage as BaTonga. The different clans traded, built alliances and fought wars, most prominently with the Maravi who attacked from north of the Zambezi river. The Maravi have remained in that territory to this day where they were joined by other groups including BaLozwi from Butua and BakaJele migrating north out of KwaZulu in the 1800s.

For *BaRozwi, BaNambiya, BaLeya, BaGwambe, BaTwamambo*, even though groups moved on and carved out separate identities, the ancestral tie to BaKalanga remained and was accepted as part of the larger identity. We believe, this is due to the smaller size of the communities and their view of overlords. Some groups easily identified with the larger identity – like BaGwambe who probably built Manyikeni. Others did not. Once they had moved on, a new identify slowly replaced the old, not always intentionally. BaGwambwe peoples kept their stone wall buildings but over time their spoken language incorporated many

BATONGA AND BAKALANGA KINGDOMS

XiTsonga words than TjiKalanga.

In trying to distinguish clans, we cannot even rely on how kin based groups were structured. Within both BaTonga and BaKalanga, we find matrilineal societies – BaLobedu of Vhembe and BaTsonga of the Nkomati, and the majority patrilineal hierarchies. The characteristic that appears to distinctly identify BaKalanga are the dry stone wall buildings which survive. They were mostly built in interior heartlands rather than the coast.

There is no question that BaKalanga ruled over larger swathes of the Lower Zambezi Valley, preferring moving from the interior to coastal lands over time. What else would explain a dominant kingdom, at various times on the banks of the Limpopo (Mapungubwe), then to the central plateau (Nzimabgwe or Kame or Danangombe) and later to the northern escarpment of the Zambezi (Mwenemutapa). Although not limited to these areas, there is no evidence of settlements along the coast for BaKalanga until the 16th century when regional dynamics began changing in rapacious ways no one could foresee. And the opposite evidence exist – BaTonga settled everywhere along the coast from the Zambezi river down as far south as Inhambane and Sofala.

BaTonga are known to have settled around the Zambezi valley as early as 400 - 500 CE. For centuries they relied on the river and its annual flooding to sustain themselves. The view that the BaTonga were largely grouped into small groups, speaking the same language with similar cultures but not united under a single ruler, is supported by the absence of a known "king of kings" in their Oral Traditions. Each clan recognised a local king, *Mpfumo* or *Hhosi*, called "Encosse" by the Portuguese. The king who may or may not have submitted to central authority of Mwenemutapa. The Kingdom of Barwe had much closer links to Mutapa whereas the Kingdom of Danda did not. The evidence of a larger groupings takes place much later in the 16th century with height of the Mwenemutapa Kingdom.

Increased trade and competition for resources exacerbated migrations over greater distances ensuring the BaTonga are found as far south as Sofala on the Indian Ocean coast by 1600. In 1506, a first hand account based in Sofala near present day Inhambane observed that BaTonga specialised in making "wine and vinegar, oil and honey, timber and tiles and also clothing..."[32] The kingdoms between the Zambezi and Limpopo would over time have a mixture of clans with some customs becoming common between groups. Having lived and fished the Zambezi river, the BaTonga from the North were known as expert fishermen of the region. They were part of *Vashambadzi* network of traders between the producers and merchants on the Indian Ocean from Kilwa, Mombasa and Persia.

4.5

MWENEMUTAPA AND THE NEW TRAVELLERS

BATONGA, BaKalanga and Muslim traders had covered the route from markets to the coast for millennia, as early as the 10th century from the records. One of the earliest Portuguese travellers to visit the Mwenemutapa interior was PC Covilha. He apparently travelled disguised as an Arab merchant. Covilha had been one of the first of his countrymen to reach Sofala after Bartholomeu

---

[32] [Documentos Sobre os Portugueses em Mocambique/Africa 1497-1840], Vol. III, p.595

MWENEMUTAPA AND THE NEW TRAVELLERS

Dias who did not go beyond the port. Covilha's letter to his king identified Sofala as the centre of the gold trade. In 1502, on his second trip, VD Gama led the first Portuguese ships into the harbour at Sofala.

The next foreigner to visit was Fernandes in 1514 – 1515. This was his second trip following his earlier attempt to get to Mwenemutapa in 1511 – 1512. Fernandes gathered reports from Swahili merchants who were trading with the Mutapas.[33] Fernandes reported to Gaspar Veloso the gold mining activities at Penhalonga, Mutari, the Revue Valley and the banks of the Pungue river. Whether Fernandes actually met the King of Manyika, or how much he traded his muskets, beads and cloth for, remains unknown.[34] Observe that the key destination was Manyika rather than the centre of Mwenemutapa Kingdom. The crucial information on trading posts in Tete and Sena is from GM Theal, which is unconfirmed.

Another important detail that Fernandes revealed to Veloso was the route to the gold mines and the Mwenemutapa Kingdom. The more direct route to the gold trading post at Manyika is through the Buzi river. Fernandes is said to have given the Sabi river (which he calls Quitengue) instead as the main route: "...the approach to this gold mining region would be best made via the river Quitengue... which flows into the sea sixteen leagues from the bar at Sofala." The distance from where the Sabi river flows into the Indian Ocean is about 80km, or 16 leagues from Sofala just north. Conferring with the map, it is clear that the southern route through the Sabi river gets to Manyika in a roundabout way. It turns out that the preference for Sabi, was due to the total control of the alternative northern route through the Pungwe river by BaTonga kings. King Nyamunda of Danda was hostile to the newly arrived.

---

[33] [Hugh Tracey, Descobridor do Monomotapa 1514 – 1515, 1940]

[34] [Documentos Sobre os Portugueses em Mocambique/Africa 1497-1840], Vol. III, p.181

Another alternative route was through the Zambezi river, much further north. The administrative documents of the day show that an attempt was made to rename the Zambezi river the *Cuama*. Unlike other place names, this one did not stick. Fernandes took a third journey to Mwenemutapa Kingdom using the Zambezi river route in 1516. The Zambezi river is located at "forty leagues" north of Sofala. The distance, equivalent to 200km, is reported by JV Almada based on accounts from Fernandes. The actual distance is much higher at 335km, but we are satisfied with 15th century estimations.

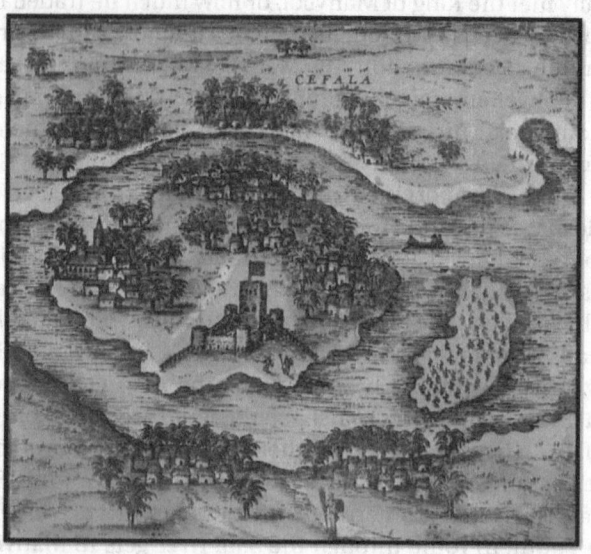

Figure 4.4: Map of ports and harbours on the east coast of Africa drawn in 1781 by Braun Georg. The original cartographical map 47cm x 32cm shows the all the ports at MOMBAZA, QVILOA and CEFALA, in Braun's spelling. The map is available at https://purl.stanford.edu/bn314rg6579

There are many anecdotes of travellers through the

MWENEMUTAPA AND THE NEW TRAVELLERS

Mwenemutapa. Fernandes's story is intriguing. He is listed in his company records as a carpenter in 1506, then as exiled in 1510, the punishment for which would be the journey into the Mwenemutapa as he was expendable. Later, as a reward for the expedition, he is back in the books listed as a carpenter and interpreter at Fort Sao Caetano in 1516, following his return. The Captain placed at Sofala includes him in his report of 1516: "(Fernandes has) already been to Benomotapa where he was held in high esteem." There are not many interesting Portuguese characters in this region who leap out of the archives than Fernandes does. Some questions about his journey remain. Where did he go, did he meet the king, can we verify the details of his travel? Hugh Tracey is resource for the untold story.[35] We conclude that, no evidence is provided that Fernandes saw Great Zimbabwe in 1511 although he spoke of it. This was probably more from second hand versions of Swahili merchants and the BaKalanga.

The immeasurable cost to the Lower Zambezi Valley peoples is evident from the financial archives of the day showing page after page of likely understated exports and departing ships. Other dedicated researchers like Hoyini Bhila have explored the imbalance with exceptional scholarship. The travellers were not only after gold but everything the kingdoms had to offer. The enslavement of local peoples was about to be multiplied and create multiplied suffering for centuries to come. Like Fernandes, another Portuguese worker stationed in Sofala from 1542 would record the events of the day for posterity. Joao Velho, certainly wanted the murder of the Muslim trader Mohammed Dao to be reported to his king. This is, not only a record of the event, but Velho's emotions as identified by Newitt.[36] We do not tell the whole tragedy again here. This is what

---

[35] [Hugh Tracey, Descobridor do Monomotapa 1514 – 1515, 1940]

[36] [Newitt, A History of Mozambique, 1995]

Velho wrote in a letter to his king.[37]
> God sees evil deeds and punishes them, but in this world, the just sometimes suffer for the sinners.

4.6
THE RISE OF THE BUTUA KINGDOM

THE Butua Kingdom based in the southwest of the Zambezi plateau, becomes more prominent in the region after the decline of Nzimabgwe beginning in 1450. Around the same time, the Kingdom of Mwenemutapa was thriving to the north, below the escarpment formed by the northern range of Fura mountains. The increased prominence of both kingdoms at that time does not imply that they had recently formed. Indeed we know that by 1450, the Torwa Dynasty had been in power at Butua for some years. Specific evidence arrives when we learn of the competition between Butua and Mwenemutapa in 1512 from the Portuguese account in the letter by Alcocova discussed earlier. In what reveals the political relationship between Mwenemutapa and Butua, no payments of tribute are mentioned.

In 1644, the capital of Butua was moved from Kame to Danangombe. A few years later in 1683, the Torwa leadership at Butua came to an end with the takeover by the *Rozvi*. BaRozvi people conquered and assimilated the Torwa-led people in Butua and went on to maintain pre-existing

---
[37] [Documentos Sobre os Portugueses em Mocambique/Africa 1497-1840], Vol. VII, p.184

THE RISE OF THE BUTUA KINGDOM

Torwa cultural practices. This is seen in the material culture from Danangombe, Naletale, Dhlo Dhlo and Zinjanja remaining unchanged after the arrival of the BaRozvi.[38] The behaviour of copying and emulating the society that has been taken over is not unique to this culture or time. The ruling Romans copied Greek philosophy and architecture after they conquered Greece. To be considered an elite in Rome, one had to speak Greek – the language of the defeated – not Latin. The Norman Conquest of England in 1066 created *beef* which until then had been known as ox or cow in Anglo-Saxon.

Whilst the archives are clear on the rival relationship between Butua and Mwenemutapa kingdoms, there were times of co-operation for political ends. This is probably due to the same origins and close relations of the Rozvi leaders of Butua and BaKalanga of Mwenemutapa. The king of Butua in 1490, Changamire, is actually an uncle of the king sitting on the throne at Mwenemutapa: Mutapa Nyahuma Mukombero.[39] The collaboration emerged when the challenge of removing the invading force of travellers who had taken over the running of the Mwenemutapa Kingdom. The Butua Kingdom, led by BaRozwi supported the push back. Curiously, the Portuguese did not attempt to the takeover of Butua Kingdom when they tried to spread their influence in the region, even though most of the gold mines were further west in Butua territories. Events proceeded the other way round. BaRozwi attacked Portuguese-run markets in Mwenemutapa territory forcing them to retreat to the coast in 1680. We delve into the Butua Kingdom in the next chapter where we learn about all the states surrounding the Mwenemutapa Kingdom: Danda, Teve, Maungwe, Birwe, Manyika and Butua.

---

[38] [Machiridza, Landscapes & Ethnicity: Hist. Archaeology of Khami, 2020]
[39] [Beach, Mutapa Dynasty: Documentary & Traditional Evidence, 1976]

5

VARIOUS KINGDOMS EMERGE AND BREAK FROM THE MUTAPA CENTRE

By the year 1500, several kingdoms had peaceful relations but were grappling for power on the Zambezi Valley. The largest states wielding the most power between the Zambezi and Limpopo were the Kingdom of Mwenemutapa, led by the *Mutapas*, and the Butua Kingdom later led by Rozwi *Changamires*. At this point, Butua can be better described as a kingdom growing in stature and influence. Contrary to the assumption that the Mwenemutapa was the centre for all the satellite and semi-independent kingdoms surrounding it, there is evidence that the Butua Kingdom was making its presence felt as a competitor to Mwenemutapa.

The death of Mutapa Nyahuma Mukembero, who sat on the throne in the years 1480 – 1490 CE, was followed by a battle for succession which could fill multiple episodes of a historical television drama. Or a tragical historical one. Or historical pastoral. It would be another hundred years before those words were printed in a separate drama of revenge by a princeling. The chronicler Alcocova tells us in 1506 of the usurper *Amyr* or *Changamire* who challenged the throne and killed the reigning Mutapa, Nyahuma Mukombero in 1490 and 22 of his children. Changamire would rule the Mwenemutapa Kingdom for four years.

Nyahuma Mukombero's surviving son, Chikuyo Chisamarengu, who had been spared because of his young age, fled to an uncle's unnamed kingdom before returning to the Mwenemutapa Kingdom. Chikuyo Chisamarengu exacted revenge, unlike the tragical-comical and endlessly dithering Hamlet who never arrived at action. Chikuyo Chisamarengu would regain the throne in 1494. The son of *Changamire the Usurper*, as he is called by historians, would rise to the throne in the Butua Kingdom led by the Torwa dynasty. We learn that the ruling elite of the kingdoms were "kinsman," confirming a view advanced in several histories. The rivalry between the two leading kingdoms would flare up in 1629 during the reign of Mutapa "Felipe" Mavura Mpande.

It is clear from these events that the Mwenemutapa Kingdom faced increasing challenges to its rule from the tribute states by the time the Portuguese arrived on the East Coast. Leading states could either see off such challenges, or they could spell the gradual beginning of the end. The breakup in 395 CE of the Eastern Roman state from the Western one – when the two sons of Theodosius ruled separately – is viewed by some historians as the beginning of the decline of Rome. Arcadius ruled the East from Constantinople and Honorius from Rome. The separation of powers indicates fragmentation within.

Other events and dates are used as an indicator of decline. History is not deterministic in occurrence. Clearly, the recorders of events capture what happened and historians of a later age define past events subjectively. The rule of Rome by a German soldier, Adoacer, who deposed Romulus Augustulus in 475 CE fits the definition of "the end" by other historians. One could also select the sacking of Rome in 410 CE as the end, the first time this happened in 800 years of that state. In the Mwenemutapa Kingdom, the conversion to Christianity by Mutapa Gatsi Rucere in 1597 could be seen as the moment when travellers to his kingdom began exercising influence. The rebellion and defeat of the Portuguese in 1632 reminds us that no single date could be considered final. Indeed, in 1693, the arriving BaRozwi drove the Portuguese out of Mwenemutapa, destroying their *feira* and pushing them back towards the Indian Ocean coast.

Before the rule of Mutapa Nyahuma Mukembero would come to an end, events taking place where the Mutapa would have considered a world away, would soon make their presence felt in his kingdom. A navigator had left the Tagus river in Portugal on the way to India. On his journey to find an alternative route, B.Dias rounded the Cape of Good Hope in 1488, eventually dropping anchor at present day Mossel Bay when the weather cooperated following several attempts.

B.Dias was one of the earliest navigators to successfully sail from the west to the east through the "current of needles," the Agulhas Current, where the cold south Atlantic meets the warm currents of the Indian Ocean. The ocean current flows southwards from India down the Mozambique and South African coast before turning back on itself and flowing eastwards. This process results in the formation of pockets of warm and salty waters in the the Atlantic ocean. The volatile structures are called *Agulhas Rings* by oceanographers. These rings of needles as the Portuguese called them, greatly increased the challenge of sailing through these waters. B.Dias called the area just south of the tip of the African continent, where he met the storms

VARIOUS KINGDOMS BREAK FROM MUTAPA

before turning back, the "Cabo Tormentosa" or Cape of Storms. His king later renamed it to the "Cabo de Boa Esperanca" or the Cape of Good Hope, for reasons we can easily guess. This name stuck.

It would take another decade for his countryman, Vasco Da Gama to arrive at the area described as "Innan Bane" in the map produced much later in 1781 called *Stati Vicini Map*. VD Gama stopped at present day Inhambane, Mozambique, on his way to India in 1498. No contact was made with the Mwenemutapa Kingdoms in the interior on the maiden voyages, although we get an account of contact with peoples on the coast. VD Gama's chronicler wrote of the "Land of Good People" and the "Copper River", which has always been known as the Vhembe River in the interior or Limpopo River as it grows and meanders to the east coast[1]:

> The arms of the people include long bows and arrows and spears with iron blades. Copper seems to be plentiful, for the people wore (ornaments) of it on their legs and arms and in their twisted hair....We stayed five days at this place, taking in water, which our visitors conveyed to our boats...We were at anchor here, near the coast, exposed to the swell of the sea. We called the country, Terra de Boa Gente (Land of Good People) and the river, Rio do Cobre (Copper River).

VD Gama made several stops including at "...this place and island of *Moncobiquy* (Mozambique) there resided a chief who had the title of Sultan, and was like a viceroy."

In subsequent visits in a few short years, a delegation from their king would be sent to Mwenemutapa Kingdom, initially requesting access to trade in the abundant ivory, gold and copper of the kingdom. The visitors had not appreciated that there were various kingdoms with different economies and ever changing relationships between the

---

[1] [Unknown, Journal of First Voyage of Vasco da Gama 1497-1499, 1898]

leaders. We meet once more the assumption of a single king, a singular people, living in a singular territory. This is the direct opposite of what they were used to back home, having fought wars with Spain.

The ascendancy of the Kingdom of Mwenemutapa at the close of 1500 CE, with Mutapa Nyahuma Mukombero in power, would usher in an expansion in the neighbouring kingdoms. We explore this era next.

Gaspar Veloso sent a letter to his king in 1512 describing the kingdoms of the Lower Zambezi Valley, based on the information collected by Antonio Fernandes.[2]

> These are the kings there are from Sofala to the mine of Monomotapa, and the things to be found in each of these kingdoms:
>
> The first king that borders with Sofala is called Mycandira and there is nothing to be had in his land save supplies and ivory.
>
> Beyond this king there is another king called the king of Mazira...(Manyika?)
>
> The king of Quytomgue lies three days journey from this other king...(This is Kiteve or Teve)
>
> The king of Embya... (This is Mbire)
>
> The king of Ynhacouce lies three days journey from this other king.
>
> The king of Ynhacouee (?) lies five days journey from this other king, he is the captain-major of the king of Menomotapa and he has great lands and in his lands they have fairs on Mondays which they call Sembaza fairs...; it is said that the fair is as big as that of Vertudes, and the only coin is gold by weight.
>
> The king of Manhiqua lies six days journey from this other king and has a great amount of gold.(Manyika)
>
> The king of Amcoce lies four days journey from this other king and he mines a great amount of gold throughout his land...(Is this Inkosi Someone?)

---

[2] [Documentos Sobre os Portugueses em Mocambique/Africa 1497-1840], Vol. III, p.181

VARIOUS KINGDOMS BREAK FROM MUTAPA

The king of Barue lies four days journey from this other king and has a great amount of gold that comes from abroad andquantities of ivory in his won land. (This is Barwe)

The king of Betomgua lies three days journey from this other king and has no gold throughout his land and is a great king.

The king of Ynhaperapara lies four days journey from this other king and mines gold throughout his land and is a great king.

The king of Boece lies five days journey from this other king and has gold that comes from abroad and is a great king.

The king of Mazofe lies four days journey from this other king and there is much gold in his land and he who mines it pays him half. (King 50% taxes)

Thence to Embire, which is a fortress of the king of Menomotapa, and is now made of stone without mortar, whic is called Camanhaya, and where he is always to be found, is a journey of five days and from there on is the kingdom of Menomotapa which is the source of the gold of all this land, and he is the greatest of all these kings, all of whom obey ihm as far as Sofala.

Beyond this king there is another who does not render him obidience and who is called the king of Butua and they lie ten days journey one from the other. He has much gold which is mined in his land along the fresh water rivers, and he is as great as the king of Menomotapa and is always at war with him.

The king of Mombara lies seven days journey from the king of Menomotapa. In this land there is much...much copper and it is from there that the copper is brought to Menomotapa...a big river lies between this king and and the king of Menomotapa whic is crossed in almadias when they come to sell their merchandise; and they set it ashore and cross again to the other side...

Monzambia , sambuks, Malindi, Kilwa, Antonio

told me he had been in all these lands and seen them...

5.1

KINGDOMS TO THE SOUTH EAST OF MWENEMUTAPA: BARWE, MANYIKA, TEVE AND DANDA

THE Kingdom of Mwenemutapa was centred in the mountain valley north of present day Harare, close to the rivers Mazoe and Dande. The administrative records repeatedly mention *Masapa* on the Mazoe river bank as the centre of the Mwenemutapa Kingdom. To the south east of Mwenemutapa were the Kingdoms of Barwe, Manyika, Teve and Danda. The map by RWG Randles shows the locations of the kingdoms in relation to Mwenemutapa from his reading of the archives.

The letter of 30 June 1513 from PV Soares to his king reports that Sofala was a peaceful place and his men lived in peace with the surrounding kings.[3] The various kingdoms allied to Mwenemutapa enjoyed relative peace although conflicts broke out especially during succession after a king had passed. Hoyini Bhila notes that the local civil wars after 1500 between Danda, Teve, Manyika, Butua and the territory actually controlled by the Mwenemutapa "were lim-

---
[3] [Soares PV, Letter from PV Soares; Documentos Sobre Vol. III, 1513]

VARIOUS KINGDOMS BREAK FROM MUTAPA

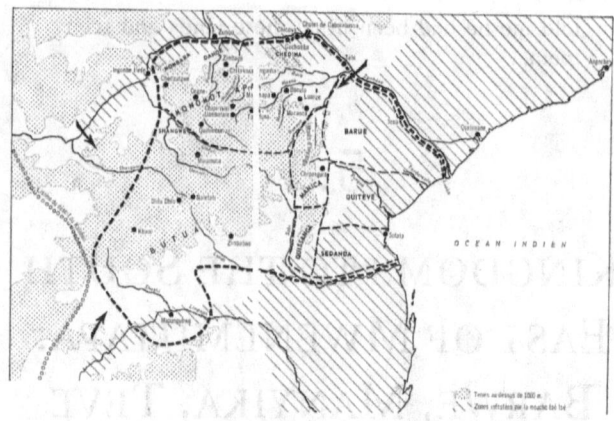

Figure 5.1: A map of the various kingdoms neighbouring Mwenemutapa – Butua, Barue, Manyika, Quiteve, Sedanda, Quissanga – with key trading centres and capitals as interpreted by the scholar WGL Randles in his Foundations of Monomotapa Empire.

ited and conventionalised affairs which did very little to alter, let alone destroy, the pattern of Manyika politics, agriculture, gold industry and trade."[4]

One conflict described in detail involves the Kingdoms of Danda, Manyika and the Mwenemutapa centre. We learn that the war between the kingdoms, with King Inhamuda of Danda on one side, the *Chikanga* of Manyika and *Monomotapa* on the other, reached its peak in 1525 – 1527 CE. The Mwenemutapa still regarded Inhamuda as his rebel provincial governor.

The internal politics of Mwenemutapa were changed permanently by the arrival of a fourth party. The kingdoms had managed the secessionist ambitions, and had found trading with the Eastern travellers from Persia lucrative and

---

[4] [Bhila, The Manyika and the Portuguese 1575-1863, 1971]

manageable. The arrival of the Portuguese on the Sofala coast would change the dynamics of the kingdoms permanently as they competed against each other with the new entrant in trading relations. The Portuguese would exploit and destroy the local dynamics.

By 1513, the newly arrived travellers increased attempts to be the only counterparty trading on the coast and vied to increase political control. Even with their armament ships which they used to destroy rival centres of commerce on the East African coast, political and economic control proved elusive to the force of canons. One of the reasons is that the political states like Danda, Teve and Butua around Sofala hinterland were arranged as autonomous states headed by the *Mambo* of the Mwenemutapa Kingdom. This decentralised structure was confusing to the Portuguese. The challenges in communicating must have contributed to the cloudy thinking. The Portuguese assumed a political hierarchy that would be similar to their own. The payment of tribute was the only familiar political structure to the travellers.

The Kingdom of Manyika was another polity which was flourishing by the sixteenth century. In the administrative records, Manyika appears to have the resources and economic trade to be independent. According to Bhila, the king could bring more than 70,000 men into the field of battle. No matter, Manyika still paid tribute to Mwenemutapa.

Settlement around the Manyika area extending to Sofala on the coast grew following the decline of Nzimabgwe from 1450. The Kingdom of Manyika arose in the highlands to the east of Nzimabgwe. The origin of the people in the Kingdom of Manyika cannot be attributed to a single group like BaKalanga or BaTonga with certainty. From the relationship Manyika enjoys with the Mwenemutapa centre, we can infer that a prince from Kingdom of Mwenemutapa was initially sent to govern lands in the far south Manyika territory. The continued paying of tribute by Manyika to

VARIOUS KINGDOMS BREAK FROM MUTAPA

the Mutapa adds evidence to this view. Over time, the Kingdom of Manyika came to increasingly govern its affairs and crowned its own kings who still had a cordial relationship with Mwenemutapa Kingdom. The leaders worked together to sell more gold.

The surrounding Kingdoms of Barwe, Teve and Danda were part of the regional trade. In what appears to have been a boom in gold mining, migration between the neighbouring kingdoms must have been on the rise. Our interest in following BaKalanga peoples in the Kingdom of Mwenemutapa will envelop the larger populations moving from one territory to another. Bhila's own view is instructive:[5]

> The fact that food supplies had to be imported from the neighbouring Kingdoms of Quiteve and Barwe suggests that the gold-mining industry had attracted large numbers of people. In fact some of the miners were outsiders – the Vatonga who lived between the Budzi and Save rivers.

The inhabitants of Danda are confirmed in this era: BaTonga, who are attracted by mining work and the growing trading markets at Masapa, Masekesa, Sena and Tete. In this period, the two key ports were at Sofala in the south and the then smaller one at Zambezi in the north. Masekesa in Manyika was by far the most important market in the 1520s.

The Kingdom of Danda was the southernmost of the kingdoms in the lower Zambezi valley. Bounded by the Sabi river to the south and the Buzi river to the north, made Danda a key player in the local trade because it controlled both routes on the waterways into the other kingdoms. When the Portuguese arrived in 1506 and attempted to insert themselves into the existing trading relations, King Nyamunda of Danda, restricted trade between the Portuguese and the Kingdom of Manyika. In the archives, King Inhamunda is called the "monster king" by another trav-

---

[5] [Bhila, The Manyika and the Portuguese 1575-1863, 1971]

eller Brito.[6] It appears this king applied his rule to his people and lands which elicited the strong reaction from bounty hunters. The Manyika "traders still had to pass through the Kingdom of Danda to sell their merchandise to the Portuguese in Sofala."[7] The Portuguese had initially reached Manyika through the longer but more navigable route of the Sabi river. From Sofala on the coast, the more direct route would be through the River Buzi cutting directly through Danda territory.

The smaller Kingdom of Teve, sandwiched between Manyika and Barwe to the north and Danda to the south, tried to remain independent. This caused strained relations between Manyika and Danda. The newly arrived had made inroads. "Quitevan opposition to Portuguese advance was not motivated by hatred for the Kingdom of Manyika. It was dictated by Quitevan interests, the desire to preserve the Kingdom inctact."[8]

The rivalry that developed between King Nyamunda with the superior Mwenemutapa–Chikanga alliance contributed to the hostile attitude of Nyamunda. The Kingdom of Danda was already under pressure from the Mutapa and Manyika alliance. We do not know the origin of these diplomatic positions. The Portuguese's ill-judged treatment of locals contributed to the hardened view by Nyamunda.[9]

To increase their influence in the region and dominate trade, the Portuguese used an existing network of traders known as *Vashambadzi*. The Portuguese would depend on this network of BaKalanga and BaTonga traders, and the old Swahili trading posts called bazaars for more than 400 years to build dominance in the region – well into the modern era. The exploitation was not only of local resources in gold mines. Increasing numbers of people were enslaved. Ex-

---

[6] [Brito, Letter from Francisco de Brito, 1519]

[7] [Bhila, The Manyika and the Portuguese 1575-1863, 1971]

[8] [Bhila, The Manyika and the Portuguese 1575-1863, 1971]

[9] [Correa, Lendas da India, 1858]

isting networks and routes were taken over to further the tearing of communities from the region. Alpers,[10] Capela[11] and others provide a more detailed history of this European episode.

When relations broke down with the King Inhamuda of Danda and his neighbours, the Portuguese probably saw an opportunity. The nature of the dispute is unknown to us. No matter, the division was to be exploited by the Portuguese to advance their objectives. They sent mercenaries to fight alongside King Nyamunda who then won a war against his rivals. There would be another war in 1518 – 1519.[12] Bhila notes that the wars peaked in 1525 and 1527 with evidence from the letters.

To get a sense of territory of the kingdoms and chieftaincies, the letter by Cristovao details the large distances travelled to see King Nyamunda.[13] We are told it was as far as the country of "Ynhambre" meaning *InhaMbire* or plain *Mbire*. The lands of the Mwenemutapa were 300 to 400 leagues (up to 1600 kilometres) inland. The Kingdom of Maungwe was so small it appears not to have had a ruler.

In time, the role of the Kingdom of Danda would be reduced as the trade moved northwards to Tete and Sena near the Zambezi river. There, the *Vashambadzi* greatly increased trade for the Portuguese. There was access to more mining output and busier travel routes. The decline of trade volumes at Sofala was so rapid that abandoning the fortification at Sofala was considered.

Bhila argues that overall, the trade in Manyika's riches was lucrative for the travellers. The Portuguese letters to authorities in Europe were written not only to report on events but also to impress upon the king the worthiness of the adventure. The reports tend emphasize conflict

---

[10] [Alpers EA, Ivory and Slaves in East Africa, 1978]

[11] [Capela Jose, Memoria a Respeito dos Escravos, 1977]

[12] [Silveira, Letter to the King, 1517]

[13] [Cristovao de Tavora, Letter from Cristova, 1518]

and moan about challenges the travellers face in the new lands. The gains, on the other hand, were serially downplayed. The letters can read like justification in the name of trade for their king. The constant drowning of the letters with problems was also meant to downplay the rewards being derived from the Danda, Manyika and Mwenemutapa. After all, any profits declared to their king would imply the need to return most of it to their leaders. Better, to over project the supposedly insurmountable problems they never met whilst attempting to extract the little gold there is to find.

Returning to the evidence we have from other spheres, in this case the Oral Traditions collected by SW Dickinson.[14] The name *Nyamunda* is frequently used in the area around Espungabeira and Chimanimani on the Buzi river. The name is often associated with the Totem *Nkomo*, used by Vandau[15] peoples of Sofala. This area was once part of the Danda Kingdom. This evidence shows that both BaTonga had occupied this region by 1500 CE and the lands to the eastern coast. The VhaNdau occupied the western interior of Danda. It is possible that both groups were part of the Danda Kingdom including the neighbouring northern Kingdom of Teve. According to Oral Traditions the largest clans to day are the *Madanda, Teve, Magova, Mashanga and Vatomboti*. VhaNdau were likely founders of the old Kingdom of Gwamba near the Sabi.

---

[14] [Dickinson, Sofala and the Rivers of Cuama, 1971]

[15] VhaNdau are a clan of the larger Vhavenda group of peoples who are descendants of many heterogeneous groups and clans including VhaFamadi, VhaLea, VhaTwamamba VhaNyai, VhaLovhedzi, VhaNdau and others.

5.2

KINGDOMS TO THE SOUTH WEST OF MUTAPA: BUTUA KINGDOM LED BY TORWA AND LATER ROZVI DYNASTY

BUTUA Kingdom is often referred to as Butua–Torwa in the literature. The leaders in Butua were called the *Torwa* which means "foreigner" in TjiKalanga language. Being the state furthest to the west from the Indian Ocean, we get limited information before 1500 in our study of the history where we approach sources from the East. This is important because were we to begin this journey of retelling the stories beginning from the west, the Congo river for instance, a whole new set of archives would need to be studied as diligently as we have done the archives from the East. Ultimately, it is the trading routes that enable us to travel into the early histories. Most preserved histories are obtained through the interactions of peoples through trade or domination of one by another, resulting in recording of events, storytelling and even the creation of myths that facilitate the process. We have approached the historical analysis of the Zambezi plateau with sources recording from the East.

In 1512, Butua was in a power struggle with the Mwenemutapa Kingdom, centred in the northeast at Musapa. There are strong indications that the gain in power for the Butua Kingdom coincides with the declining power of

KINGDOMS SOUTH WEST OF MUTAPA: BUTUA

the famous Mwenemutapa Kingdom. We also know that the leaders at Butua had probably taken over that kingdom too as they were referred to as foreigners. Up until 1690s, most mentions of Butua coincide with Mwenemutapa as the main rivalry in northern Zambezi. No direct war was mentioned but the competitive positions are evident. There was no payment of tribute from Butua to Mwenemutapa, which was the norm for the surrounding kingdoms. Manyika, Danda, Teve or Barwe kingdoms, which emerge through secession by sons of the ruling Mwenemutapa elites, appear as many times the Mutapa kingdom in the archives through events including during trade negotiations, payment of taxes and minor disputes.

When Nzimabgwe went into decline around 1450, Kame was already under the leadership of the Torwa dynasty. We know that the capital was moved from Kame to Danangombe in 1644. A few years after, a people arriving from the north, known as BaRozwi challenged the Torwa for the leadership of the Butua Kingdom and won a decisive battle in 1683. Another settlement, similar in style to both Kame and Danangombe was built at Naletale. The aim by scholars to fully understand the relationship between the Torwa and BaRozwi is now focused on the four sites at Kame, Danangombe, Naletale and Zinjanja. BaRozwi, who were BaKalanga would go on to forge new kingdoms to the east and as far south as the Thukela.

The Arab Navigator and Cartographer Ahmad Ibn Majid wrote of sailing to the African coastline. His *The Useful Information on the Principles and Rules of Navigation* was written around 1490 and provides a guide on sailing using the stars. Even those who do not maintain a curiosity with archives or seek historical knowledge, will be instantly familiar with the name Vasco Da Gama. His achievement of rounding the Cape of Torrents is almost a refrain. What is less known is that Ahmad Ibn Majid's literature on navigation made Da Gama's navigation to India possible. The

VARIOUS KINGDOMS BREAK FROM MUTAPA

Ruler of Malindi provided Da Gama with a pilot for the voyage.

The route from Malindi in present day Kenya to Calicut, India was not known to Da Gama. His cartographer was useless beyond this point, which is when he turned to Ahmad Ibn Majid's cartography and local Malindi navigators. Such detail is easily missed in historical texts when reading with prior assumptions. Indeed, some eliminate it altogether. Da Gama's own logs of the journey mention that he enlisted the help of an "Arab Mariner" to complete his journey to India arriving 20 May 1498. The sources are not unanimous in the account of Da Gama's voyage to India. Others name the Malindi pilot as Malemo. Some judge this to be a misspelling of Muslim. Other sources contend the pilot was Gujirati stationed at Malindi. There is no debate on the writings of Ahmad Ibn Majid for his contribution to the navigation journey to India.

To round the southernmost tip of the African continent, Da Gama relied on earlier journeys of his countryman B. Dias who made various attempts from 1488 to traverse the Cape of Torrents. That name is mistranslated from its "Agulhas Current" name into torrents instead of needles. The southernmost tip of land beyond which the currents are found was renamed the Cape of Good Hope. Traversing these waters presented a challenge to European navigators but in East Africa, merchants and sailors had been trading with China and Persia for centuries.

Ahmad Ibn Majid writes:[16]

> This bay is long, it originates in the Nile, Egypt valley. Here at that distance. The majority of those living between Sofala and Kilwa are infidels, who are called to arms, according to the name of Muna-Batur (Mwene Batua), a great king...He owns the centre of Sofala, because he governs the eastern part of this region...

---

[16] [Ahmad Ibn Majid, Book of Info. on Principles of Navigation, c.1490]

KINGDOMS SOUTH WEST OF MUTAPA: BUTUA

Tawanda Mukwende in his study of the archaeology of the Khami and the Butua State[17] describes the location of Butua as covering a large area that included modern day southwestern Zimbabwe, northeast Botswana and northern South Africa. The picture we form in our minds of this large kingdom and its location coincides with the described location of a state centred at Kame that thrived from 1400 – 1680 CE. The capital was later moved from Kame to the east at Danangombe.

The Kings of Butua Kingdom had the title of *Changamire*. The first ruling Changamire was the name of a specific king. Later on, the name would transform into a title and be used for kings in a process similar to how Caesar became Kaiser in the 19th century.

The naming convention of using Changamire has created confusion in the reading of the archives. Trying to match the archives with the Oral Tradition passed down by generations presents challenges. When a king is mentioned by title alone, such as *Changamire*, a closer study of the dates of reign are required clue to identify which king is sitting on the throne. There is further confusion in that the records can attribute the title *Changamire* to a king not associated with the Butua Kingdom. A careful study of context helps us resolve this. We leave historical gaps filled with the silence they emit, rather than fill them.

Butua rejected continuing rule from the Mwenemutapa; It appears that the Butua Kingdom and the Kingdom of Danda tried to gain independence in the running of their affairs. Bhila informs us that King Nyamunda of the Kingdom of Danda, based near the Buzi river and bounded to the south by the Save river, was in full revolt at leadership from the Mwenemutapa centre.[18]

Conflicts and civil wars, which were limited and not destructive, continued between the Mwenemutapa and the

---

[17] [Mukwende, The Archaeology of Khami and the Butua State, 2020]

[18] [Bhila, The Manyika and the Portuguese 1575-1863, 1971]

VARIOUS KINGDOMS BREAK FROM MUTAPA

Butua–Torwa succession in the period 1494 – 1512 CE. Different states formed alliances. The Mwenemutapa was in alliance with the Chikanga. The King of Manyika was at war with another tributary state, the Kingdom of Danda led by King Nyamunda, written as *Inhamunda* in Portuguese records. The conflict was observed in the diminished flow of gold to Sofala which was recorded by administrators on the coast.

There was far more external contact with the Kingdom of Mwenemutapa than Butua based on the volume of written records. Documentary archives are but one of the sources of evidence in our research. Archaeological findings and the Traditions are rich sources of what we know about Butua. Although relevant to a later period in the 17th century, the Butua Kingdom was on the rise. Butua eventually became one of the dominant powers in the region as Mutapa declined from encroachment. Chinese Ming porcelain and Arabian pottery together with other artefacts were excavated at the Butua capital at Kame, offering evidence of trading relations. More recent archaeological studies have identified more towns that were part of the Butua Kingdom: Naletale, and Danangombe (now Dhlodhlo).

5.3

THE DAWN OF 1500 CE BRINGS A SCRAMBLE AND THE GIBBON DECLINE AND FALL

THE Eastern states under Roman rule, whose capital was based at Constantinople, became distinctly separated in 395 CE from the Western states ruled from Rome. That followed the death of the leader Theodosius, as his sons split the polity to rule separately in the East and West. In North Africa, Roman rule based at Alexandra in Egypt was abandoned a few years later in 430 CE. In the year 476 CE, the last local emperor ruled before a German soldier overthrew him. And, in the year of 410 CE, Rome was sacked for the first time in 800 years, a sign of a weakened state which soon ceased to exist as an identifiable unit. Which year would you pick to mark the beginning of the decline and fall of Rome: 395, 410, 430 or 476 CE? Scholars face the same choice, backing it up with evidence and force of argument, nothing more.

To determine the beginning of the decline, not only do we have to choose a time we deem fit, but with more difficulty, we have to define what a declining kingdom is. Would decline be defined by loss in a major battle, an invasion or the death of a long-reigning and unifying leader, failure to successfully levy and collect taxes from citizens near the capital and in the outposts of the state, or a splitting of the territory in succession disputes? As the history of Rome shows, there are many possible events which lead to disintegration which are all candidates for defining a decline.

The decline of the Mwenemutapa Kingdom cannot be placed precisely in time or meaning. From our research, we view the beginning of the decline of the kingdom as the year 1623. This was during the reign, or close to the end of the reign of Mutapa Gatsi Rusere. Mutapa Gatsi Rusere conceded too much ground in the treaties with the Portuguese; he was baptised and was said to have been a ruler only in name. With the help of the Butua Kingdom, he drove the Portuguese to the coast and regained his kingdom, but the internal structures and regional hierarchy had been shattered. Power depends not only on its exercise, but the imagination of its exercise, especially by outsiders. As the chart showing the genealogy of Mutapa at the beginning of the book shows, every Mutapa after 1623 has a Portuguese baptism name appended. Symbolic. It provides the imagery of a state in decline and ruled by visitors. We need only fill in the events that follow to understand how the kingdom faced momentous times.

The Portuguese first arrived and made contact with BaKalanga in 1505. We get various accounts from the written archives including Santos (1609),[19] Barros (1778),[20] Barbossa (1892)[21] and Correa (1869).[22] The Portuguese arrivals were informed of the most powerful leader, "Lord of the Lands," also called "Prince of the Realm" or "He Who Takes All," in TjiKalanga "Nhu Unotapa" which they understood and wrote as *Monomotapa*. Within a hundred years, they would take control of the eastern part of the region.

We get further details of precipitous moments before the challenge from outsiders for the Kingdom of Mwenemu-

---

[19] [Santos, Ethiopia Oriental e Historia do Oriente, 1609]

[20] [Barros, Da Asia: Dos Feitos, Que os Portugueses Fizeram..., 1778]

[21] [Barbossa, Esmeralso Orbis, 1892]

[22] [Correa, Lendas da India, 1869]

tapa increased. One account comes from a priest who was based in India but was sent to visit BaKalanga in the interior. Father Silveira was well received although he was later killed due a disagreement with the Mambo of BaKalanga around 1560 which was used as a further reason to control the local kingdoms.

This instalment has focused on the years 900 – 1500 CE. In the next of this series we will show the battle for the chiefdoms, kingdoms and independent states of BaKalanga and BaTonga after 1500. The death of Mwenemutapa Nogomo Makunzagutu in 1597, and subsequent coronation of Mutapa Gatsi Rusere certainly signalled irreversible change. Power and control of Mutapa kingdoms did not come at once. There was a rebellion in 1631 with the alliance of the Maravi arriving north of the Zambezi to drive out the Portuguese, retreats to consolidate and eventual capitulation to further incursions by the travellers firmly placed near the ports. This is before we mention the impact of Christianity on a spiritual level to the people of the region.

As has been observed repeatedly in other worlds, this was no exchange of one set of beliefs for another but a complete rewiring and surrendering of the natural order. A new way of life, one that was unknown and had to be learned. The people's ability to imagine, dream and believe had to find a new structure in the arriving order and chaos. In the unpredictable ways events play out, the heartlands of ancient Butua and Mutapa kingdoms, would fall to travellers arriving much later, in 1652, having landed as far south at the Salt river, rather than the more recently arrived at the Save or Zambezi river. One can imagine the Mutapas looking east and dealing with challenges in that direction.

The people of the region were increasingly on the move. We will explore how BaKalanga, specifically AmaLala ended up beyond the Phongolo river with in the Ndwandwe Kingdom which later became the KwaZulu Kingdom. Following the breakup of the Ndwandwe Kingdom in 1858, after

VARIOUS KINGDOMS BREAK FROM MUTAPA

the death of King Zwide, his generals would march north, Manukosi founding the southern Gasa Kingdom, Mzilikazi founding AmaNdebele Kingdom and Msane and Jele would march north past the Zambezi river into present day Zambia and Malawi.

Kinsmen and courtiers in the history of the 19th century whom very little has been written about will be brought light. We will explore the genealogy of the Zikode Dynasty and the families of Gazithi, Ncayi-ncayi, Dlamini or Jamene, Magidjane Tavedi or Thevede, Madumana Mlotse and Dongwa Mabesa, who by all accounts were part of the royal family of Gasa.[23] We chronicle the lineages and interactions with Manukosi, Ngungunyane, Shaka, Dingane, Ngwane, Mziliwegazi or Mzilikazi and Zwangendaba among others.

---

[23] [Liesegang, Internal Gaza Kingdom, Mozambique 1840 – 1895, 1981]

SOURCES IN THE HISTORY OF THE GREAT ZAMBEZI

THIS historical account of BaKalanga, BaTonga and the Great Zambezi kingdoms rests on three foundations of evidence that we analysed and critiqued before building a depth of understanding of the events by corroborating across the sources. Our view is built on the documental evidence, archaeological evidence and the Oral Traditions recorded.

The history of BaKalanga and the various kingdoms in its dominion relies on archived records of the era, both first hand accounts and information relayed to authorities sometimes far and removed from the location of events. The letters and administrative records of prices, trade goods and legal disputes recorded are immensely valuable even if lacking in texture and ethnography of local peoples. The documents tend to be overly focused on trade, what the Portuguese can extract and what they report to their king.

We rely on archaeological evidence from various scholars who are publishing new works analysing the early communities in the Zimbabwe plateau. Beach, Randles, Morais and Huffman were among the early researchers in the late 1970s with expansion in research sites and methods. The added collaborative approach from scholars including Chirikure, Pikirayi, Machiridza, Mosothwane, Matenga, Pollard and many others grew. New scholarship and depth of knowledge has added a volume of detailed analysis of various aspects of Mapela Hill (1200 CE), Mapungubwe (1200 CE), Great Zimbabwe (1250 CE), Khami (1400 CE) or Mwenemutapa Kingdom (1450 CE). The focus is no longer on Great Zimbabwe alone. New knowledge and findings can stand on their own without requiring Great Zimbabwe to be the anchor.

The geography, weather, metallurgy, pottery, trade in goods and archaeological links to Persia and India are all investigated from first principles. The improvement in technology and decline in prices of technology, means that archaeological evidence has added a larger weight as the second wing of evidence. Notwithstanding the degradation of the important historical sites from looting, or shortcomings from the early "archaeological expeditions" which removed artefacts considered African, thus "foreign" to an old African kingdom like Great Zimbabwe, the remaining monuments still yield thousands of objects for examination and study. In 1893 Theodore Bent removed objects he considered African including "pottery, spindle whorls, metal objects" and "focused his attention on soapstone birds, imported ceramics and beads."[24] Definitely bent! The whole move to return artefacts to their rightful owners will only accelerate the process of retelling the history with evidence in tow.

From what remains, caution should still apply to interpretation of objects as demonstrated by Chiripanhura that "material objects are indeed reluctant witnesses to the past."[25] There is only so much we can find out from static objects whose use sometimes evades us, let alone their importance to the dynamism of a society more than 500 years ago.

The Oral Tradition or Traditions refers to testimony transmitted by word of mouth from one generation to another. Various medium are used for storing, enriching and passing information. Songs, poems, theatre, beliefs, practices, customs and many other media all are used capture knowledge in societies. In the writing of the history of the Lower Zambezi, Traditions were previously overlooked resulting in the distorted accounts. New scholars and readers

---

[24] [Chiripanhura, Archaeological Collections Research: Zimbabwe, '18],p.31

[25] [Chiripanhura, Archaeological Collections Research: Zimbabwe, '18]

of first hand account including this author are retelling the history and separating myth from factual accounts. Had the "early historians" used the available documentary evidence side by side with oral accounts they would have corroborated some histories, explained beliefs within a context, and limited inaccurate or incomplete knowledge from being passed down the generations.

In this historical account, we evaluate and incorporate Oral Traditions, following in the footsteps of new scholars from the region. When used together, a more informed understanding emerges whilst accepting the gaps that exist. As a warning, Oral Traditions are not without their challenges, the most common being the "feedback" mechanism. Published materials can find their way into common local knowledge and is chronicled as ancient oral history with all the distortions and errors at source. As for recorders of the Oral Traditions, the recorded accounts are only valuable as unaltered and uninterpreted first hand accounts. David Beach accurately observed of one recorder of Mutapa Traditions, DP Abraham: "In some cases, it is difficult to separate the researcher in his role as an unwitting informant from his role as a collector of data."[26] Nothing more could prove that history is a process that is alive and living. It is only the ink dries up in the texts, not knowledge.

The Traditions recorded by Vusamazulu Credo Mutwa, Pathisa Nyathi, FM Vilakazi, DN Beach, Ismael Mwale in Margaret Read, Msebensi Zwane to Albert Hlongwane in Van Warmelo, to name but a few, are some of the most fascinating historical accounts one can read. A presence and proximity is felt by the reader of these first hand accounts from the elders who have seen many different times and events in their lifetimes including the stories they were told by their elders.

Another source of knowledge for our historical account

---

[26] [Beach, Mutapa Dynasty: Documentary & Traditional Evidence, 1976]

are the proverbs and sayings which have survived for millennia. Careful interpretation is required as different proverbs can be adapted for contemporary times. African historians agree on the ancient sources of most sayings and the wisdom they have carried down the generations. The Zimbabwean historian Pathisa Nyathi, in his collection of cultural stories, *Zimbabwe's Cultural Heritage*, recalls the proverb used by the BaTonga peoples who lived on both banks of the Zambezi river and were known to use it for transportation in their canoes.

Bwato tabulindi muntu, bulindilwa aachito.

The message is clear to those who require transportation on the river: "The owner of the canoe does not wait for intending travellers, instead, travellers should wait for (the canoe owner) at the crossing point."[27] The *chito* is conveniently the shallow areas of the river providing access.

---

[27] [Pathisa Nyathi, Zimbabwe's Cultural Heritage, 2005]

1500 CE: SCRAMBLE AND GIBBON DECLINE

> **Nota Bene (NB); Buka Kahle (BK):** The documentary evidence together with accounts from the Ora Tradition have created a variety of spellings of the names, to the extent that one cannot sometimes recognise when talking about the same peoples. Without trying to standardise everywhere, especially in cases where the similarity is obvious, and for correct historical representation, in this work we have attempted to harmonise names for ease of reading. Here are some variations of the same names that should be noted:
>
> **BaKalanga** – variations include BaKaranga, Kalanga or Karanga, Khalaka or Mokhalaka, "Mocaranga" or "Vealanga" in the Portuguese documents, and so on
>
> **BaLozwi** – BaLozi, BaRozwi, Baloyi, "Barobze"; a clan belonging to the larger BaKalanga group; they were also known as the Torwa Dynasty
>
> **BaLemba** – BaLembya, BaLeya, VhaLea; a BaKalanga clan; **BaNambiya** – variations include BaNambya; a BaKalanga clan
>
> **King** – Mambo, Mutapa, Chikanga, Chibundule, Changamire
>
> **Mwenemutapa** – Inperio do Manamotapa, Imperio del Monomotapa, Benomotapam, Munhumutapa, Mutapa
>
> **Chibundule** – a Torwa king; **Changamire** – a BaRozwi king

The bibliography includes a good proportion of the sources that readers can use to dip further into the well of BaKalanga and the peoples of the Lower Zambezi Valley. Certainly, most of the first hand accounts and sources have been covered. In this short review of sources, we can highlight a few works that the reader can begin with. For the meat, turn to Moyo's *The Rebirth of BuKalanga, 2012*, Pikirayi's *Great Zimbabwe*, Bhila's *The Manyika and the Portuguese 1575 – 1863, 1971* and JD Barros and DD Couto's *Documents on the Portuguese in Mozambique and Central Africa 1497 – 1840*.

For the bones and marrow, that additional nourishment hidden dipper within, some scholars have spent enormous amount of time on the topic that it would be remiss not to feast on their findings. These various academic papers will introduce the subject without a single paper giving the broad overview you might require, but without them the reader will not be as nourished having gone through the meaty part. Beach's *A Zimbabwe Past: Shona Dynastic Histories and Oral Traditions, 1994*, Chirikure's *Mapela Hill*, Huffman's *The Leopards Kopje Tradition, 1974*, Hamilton, Mbenga and Ross's *South Africa Vol.I From Early Times to 1885* all offer rich analysis, and there are many more to name here.

QUESTIONS IN THE HISTORY OF THE GREAT ZAMBEZI

READING historical archives, first hand accounts, important contributions from secondary researchers, even from the misguided interpretation works, countless articles and commentaries online, detailed archaeological field work and findings from dedicated scholars, and the painstakingly recorded and documented Oral Traditions provide a rich resource of information.

The abundance of sources does not diminish the difficulty of assembling the sources, getting access to sources – a task being made ever easier by advances in technology or the gaps in the information provided by the sources. Reading the various works provides such a joy, as one is enlightened by events past, especially from the first hand accounts. An insight from dedicated researchers can provide the spark for the current generation of researchers like me. We are comfortable with gaps in the histories, and make no attempt to fill a void without evidence. As researchers everywhere will know, the more one reads and researches, the more questions arise than answers. Luckily, more sources appear but the reader needs to limit the scope of his research. Here then are some questions we would have loved to pursue, and there are plenty of papers to get started but was beyond scope.

i. A kingdom by the name of Chicova was known well enough to appear on Maps and texts dating to early 1500s. The Kingdom of Chicova was north of Manyika, west of Mutapa but bounded to the west by Butua. We do not find more than a mere mention of this kingdom and their ruler and we wonder if he was one of the Mwenemutapa Kings? Was he the *Mutapa* Chikuyo Chisamarengu who ousted and ruled after *Changamire the Usurper*?

ii. The Torwa dynasty who were leaders of the Butua Kingdom in the southwest of present day Zimbabwe can be traced to BaKalanga identity. They ceased to be the leaders of Butua on the arrival of a peoples called BaRozwi. This is also a clan of BaKalanga. Given both clans are Bakalanga, at least in origin, what led to the takeover of the Butua Kingdom with the capi-

VARIOUS KINGDOMS BREAK FROM MUTAPA

tal at Kame by BaRozwi and the move to a new capital at Danangombe, leaving gold mining and land access aside? Was there any historical succession conflict or rivalry for the throne being revisited? Or was it a new people arriving in new lands and ceasing control as history has shown repeatedly? This history is incomplete.

iii. The evidence is overwhelming and clearly indicates that Nzimabgwe, Butua, Mwenemutapa, Teve, Danda and other kingdoms in the region had been trading with Sofala, Kilwa, Malindi, Mombasa, Sassanid Persia, Goa in India and Ming China. Did the early travellers reach Benguera and the Congo Kingdom, Kush, Aksum, Songhai or Mali along the West Coast?

iv. How much can we lend to the view that BaLemba, BaNyayi and VhaVenda ruled their own kingdoms which were part of the larger BaKalanga group and identity, whose centre was at Mwenemutapa from 1500 onwards.

v. Genealogy of Mutapas? We have put one together from all the sources we have read but slightly surprised that no one has published a single unified version yet. A few versions exists out there but not with the chronology we provide.

vi. There is enough evidence to support the view that some BaKalanga moved from Great Zimbabwe to Khami, not direct and convincing but enough support for that idea. Not enough evidence exists to support the view that the Mwenemutapa Kingdom was formed from the remains of Great Zimbabwe. David Beach. Chirikure. Ndzimu-Unami Moyo. The debate goes on.

vii. Mfecane is not covered you say? What does that word mean? Mfe-what? Where did it originate from? Has it been repeated so many times you now take it as fact yet cannot point to its origin, not in songs and poems of the people of the Pongolo and Thukela? Have you asked your grandmother? Professor M. Mbenga at the University of North West, South Africa, has written extensively to dispel the use of that word and its warped history by taking readers through the history of 1800s south of the Limpopo. We cover the period after 1500 CE in the next volume. Only the events presented from archived records will make an appearance without resorting to invented words that explain everything happening everywhere. Africa has always been a country *bathong*!

PICTURE CREDITS ©

1. Map of the Kingdom of Mwenemutapa and surrounding kingdoms [Alpers, Dynasties of the Mutapa-Rozwi Complex, 1970]- *Courtesy ©EA Alpers* x
2. Chronology of the Period 200 – 1700 AD- *(Source: Compiled by the Author)* xi
3. Period of Reign in the Kingdom of Mwenemutapa (*Source: Compiled by the author*) xii

1.1 A few Early Farming Community sites around present day Zimbabwe [Chirikure, Manyanga, Pollard, Zimbabwe Culture, 2014] ©Creative Commons License.-*Chirikure at al.* 6
1.2 Distribution of Early Farming Community settlements in Zimbabwe [Chirikure, Manyanga, Pollard, Zimbabwe Culture, 2014] Courtesy ©Creative Commons License-*Chirikure et al.* 10
1.3 Sketch by Van Waarden and Mosothwane of the burial at Mathangwane [Van Waarden, Mosothwane, Leopard's Kopje Burial, 2013]- *Courtesy ©Van Waarden and Mosothwane* 17
1.4 The restored nine pots recovered from the burial at Mathangwane from [Van Waarden, Mosothwane, Leopard's Kopje Burial, 2013]- *Courtesy ©Van Waarden and Mosothwane* 19
1.5 Remaining monuments of villages and royal courts in the old kingdoms of the Lower Zambezi Valley- *Courtesy ©Dzowa* 26

PICTURE CREDITS ©

2.1 Artefacts recovered in 1933 from Mapungubwe-*Courtesy ©University of Pretoria* 32

3.1 Zimbabwe soapstone birds recovered from Nzimabgwe-*Courtesy ©National Museums and Monuments of Zimbabwe* 49

3.2 The narrow passage in the Great Enclosure at Nzimabgwe from both a photograph and an artist's rendering of how it looked-*Courtesy ©Dzowa and ©Ledama* 52

3.3 The Great Enclosure at Great Zimbabwe-*Courtesy ©Dzowa* 53

3.4 The Conical Tower in the Great Enclosure and a Main Entrance to the 13th century Kingdom of Nzimabgwe-*Courtesy ©Dzowa* 54

4.1 The Indian Ocean Route to Mutapa States and India via Mombasa Courtesy [Dickinson, Sofala and the Rivers of Cuama, 1971]-*Courtesy ©RW Dickinson* 95

4.2 Map of Mutapa States-*Courtesy ©Google Maps* 101

4.3 Impero del Monomotapa e Stati Vicini of 1781; The Map of the Kingdom of Mwenemutapa and Neighbouring States of 1781; ©Creative Commons Courtesy The Dr. Oscar I. Norwich Collection of Maps of Africa and its Islands 1486 –ca.1865; David Rumsey Map Centre Stanford University Libraries-*Venice Bellin; Jacques Nicholas 1703-1772* . . 111

4.4 Map of ports and harbours on the east coast of Africa drawn in 1781 by Braun Georg; ©Creative Commons Courtesy Norwich I.; Pam Colbe and Jeffrey C Stone. Norwich's Maps of Africa: An Illustrated and Annotated Carto-Bibliography. 2nd ed. & rev and edited by Jeffrey C Stone Vt.; Terra Nova press; 1997; map 0332; p.380-*Braun Georg* 120

PICTURE CREDITS ©

5.1 Cahiers d' Etudes: La Fondation de L'Impire du Monomotapa by WGL Randles [Randles, L'empire du Monomotapa du XV au XIX siecle, 1975]- *Courtesy ©WGL Randles* 132

BIBLIOGRAPHY

[A.H.M, Cod.2-437 FE 6, fol. 145, JSN de Andrade to Monteiro, Massangano, 1836] ***A.H.M*** Cod.2-437 FE 6, fol. 145, J Sousa Nunes de Andrade to Monteiro, Massangano; 11/11/1836

[A.H.M, Cod.2-437 FE 6, fol. 48v, Andrade to Monteiro, Massangano, 1836] ***A.H.M*** Cod.2-437 FE 6, fol. 48v, Andrade to Monteiro, Massangano; 12/12/1836

[A.H.M, Gov. Geral, 12, corresp. rec. de Sofala, G Nunes to GCG Botelo, no.23, 1827] ***A.H.M*** Gov. Geral, 12, corresp. rec. de Sofala, G Nunes to GCG Botelo, no.23; 23 February 1827

[Ahmad Ibn Majid, Book of Info. on Principles of Navigation, c.1490] ***Ahmad Ibn Majid*** Book of Useful Information on the Principles and Rules of Navigation; c.1490

[Alpers EA, Ivory and Slaves in East Africa, 1978] ***EA Alpers*** Ivory and Slaves in East Central Africa, Africa and Asian Studies; 1978

[Alpers, Dynasties of the Mutapa-Rozwi Complex, 1970] ***Alpers EA***; Dynasties of the Mutapa-Rozwi Complex; Journal of African History; 1970

[Alpers, The Role of the Yao in the Development of Trade in East Africa, 1966] ***Alpers EA*** The Role of the Yao in the Development of Trade in East Central Africa 1698 – c1850, PhD London; 1966

[Axelson, South East Africa 1488 – 1530, 1940] ***Axelson E.*** South East Africa 1488 – 1530, Longmans; 1940

[Barnes JA, Politics in a Changing Society, 1954] ***Barnes JA*** Politics in a Changing Society. A Political History of the Ft Jameson Ngoni, Oxford University Press; 1954

[Beach D, A Zimbabwe Past: Shona Dynastic History and Oral Traditions, 1994] ***D Beach***; A Zimbabwe Past: Shona Dynastic History and Oral Traditions; 1994

[Beach, Mutapa Dynasty: Documentary & Traditional Evidence, 1976] ***DN Beach***; The Mutapa Dynasty: A comparison of Documentary and Traditional Evidence, History in Africa; 1976

[Bhila, The Manyika and the Portuguese 1575-1863, 1971] ***HHK Bhila*** The Manyika and the Portuguese 1575-1863, PhD Thesis SOAS London; 1971

BIBLIOGRAPHY

[Bhila, Trade and Politics in the Shona Kingdom: The Manyika, 1982] ***HHK Bhila*** Trade and Politics in the Shona Kingdom: The Manyika and Their Portuguese and African Neighbours, 1575-1902, London; 1982

[Boxer and Azevedo, Fort Jesus and The Portuguese in Mombasa 1593 - 1729, 1960] ***Boxer CR and Azevedo Carlos de*** Fort Jesus and The Portuguese in Mombasa 1593 – 1729, London; 1960

[Braudel F, A History of Civilisations, 1995] ***Graudel F*** A History of Civilisations, Penguin; 1995

[Bryant AT, Olden Times in Natal and Zululand, 1956] ***AT Bryant***; Olden Times in Natal and Zululand; 1929; Struik Reprint 1956

[Calabrese, Interregional Integration in Southern Africa: Zhizo, 2000] ***Calabrese JA*** interregional Integration in southern Africa: Zhizo and Leopards Kopje Relations in Northern South Africa, Southwestern Zimbabwe and Eastern Botswana AD 1000 – 2000, The African Archaeological Review, 17 (4), 183 –210; 2013

[Capela Jose, Memoria a Respeito dos Escravos, 1977] ***Capela Jose*** Memoria a Respeito dos Escravos e Trafico da Escravatura entre a Costa d' Africa e o Brazil Apresentada a Real Academia das Ciencias de Lisboa; 1975

[Carruthers, Mapungubwe: Historical & Contemporary Analysis, 2006] ***Carruthers J*** Mapungubwe: A Historical and Contemporary Analysis of a World Heritage Cultural Landscape, University of South Africa; 2006

[Casson L, Periplus Maris Erythreai, 1989] ***Casson L*** Periplus Maris Erythreai Sea, Princeton University Press; 1989

[Casson, Periplus Maris Erythreai, 1989] ***Periplus Maris Erythreai*** Periplus Maris Erythreai, Princeton Press; 1989

[Chami Felix, Roman beads from the Rufiji Delta, Tanzania, 1999] ***Felix Chami*** Roman beads from the Rufiji Delta, Tanzania: First incontrovertible archaeological link with the Periplus. Current Anthropology, 40 (2), p.237-241; 1999

[Chami Felix, The Tanzanian Coast in the First Millenium AD, 1994] ***Felix Chami*** The Tanzanian Coast in the First Millennium AD: An archaeology of the iron working farming and farming communities, Studies in African Archaeology; 1994

[Chirikure and Pikirayi, Debating Great Zimbabwe, 2011] ***Chirikure Innocent and Pikirayi Shadreck*** Debating Great Zimbabwe, Azania Archaeological Research in Africa, Vol. 46, No. 2; 2011

[Chirikure and Pikirayi, Inside and Outside the Dry Stone Walls, 2015] ***Chirikure Shadreck and Pikirayi Innocent*** Inside and Outside the Dry Stone Walls: Revisiting the Material Culture of Great Zimbabwe, Antiquity 82, 2008, 976 –993; 2015

[Chirikure, Manyanga, Pikirayi, Pathways of Sociopolitial Complexity, '13] ***Chirikure Shadreck, Manyanga Munyaradzi, Pikirayi Innocent, Pollard Mark*** New Pathways of Sociopolitical Complexity in Southern Africa, Springer; 2013

[Chirikure, Manyanga, Pollard, Zimbabwe Culture, 2014] ***Chirikuye, Manyanga, Pollard et al.***; Zimbabwe Culture before Mapungubwe: new evidence from Mapela Hill, South-Western Zimbabwe, University of Cape Town; 2014

[Chiripanhura, Archaeological Collections Research: Zimbabwe, '18] ***Chiripanhura Pauline*** Archaeological Collections as a Prime Research Asset: Objects and Great Zimbabwe's Past, PhD, University of Cape Towns; 2018

BIBLIOGRAPHY

[Chittick N, Kilwa: An Islamic Trading City on the East African Coast, 1974]
Chittick N Kilwa: An Islamic trading city on the East African Coast, the Finds, British Institute of East Africa; 1974

[Christian Isendahl, Angoche: Link of the Zambezian Gold Trade, Undated]
Cristian Isendahl Angoche: an Important Link of the Zambezian Gold Trade, University of Gothenburg; Undated

[Cobbing J, Review of The Deal will Arise: Nongqawuse, 1989] *J Cobbing*; Review of The Dead Will Arise: Nongqawuse and the Great Xhosa Cattle-Killing Movement of 1856 to 1857

[Cobbing J, The Ndebele under the Khumalo 1820 -1896, 1976] *J.Cobbing*; The Ndebele under the Khumalo, 1820 - 1896, PhD University of Lancaster; 1976

[Da Gama, First Voyage of Vasco Da Gama 1497-1499, 2014] *VD Gama*; The Project Gutenberg Ebook of a Journal of the First Voyage of Vasco Da Gama 1497 - 1499; Author Unknown XCIX-MDCCCXCVIII; Translator E Ravenstein;http://www.pgdp.net; eBook 2014

[Dickinson, Sofala and the Rivers of Cuama, 1971] *RW Dickinson*; Sofala and the Rivers of Cuama: Crusade and Commerce in SE Africa 1505 – 1595, PhD, Univesiy of Cape Town, 1971

[Duarte Barbossa, Livro de Duarte Barbossa, c.1516] *Duarte Barbossa* Livro de Duarte Barbossa, two volumes reprinted in 1996; circa 1516

[Erskine, Third and Fourth Journeys in Gaza Mozambique 1873-1874, 1878]
Erskine St Vincent Third and Fourth Journeys in Gaza or Southern Mozambique 1873-1874 in R.G.S No.48, London; 1878

[Evans and Webster, Archaeology of Ancient Mexico, 2001] *Evans Susan and Webster David* Archaeology of Ancient Mexico and Central American Encyclopaedia, New York, Garland Publishing; 2001

[Galvao, Diario das Viagens, 1935] *Manuel da Silva Galvao*; Diario das Viagens, in Dias Carvalho's Fontes para a Historia; also see Botelho Xavier, Memoria Estatica Sobre os Dominios Portugueses na Africa Oriental, Lisbon; 1935

[Garlake Peter, An Investigation of Manekweni, Mozambique, 1976] *Garlake Peter* An Investigation of Manekweni, Mozambique, Azania Archaeological Research in Africa, Volume 11, Issue 1; 1976

[Giddens Anthony, The Constituion of a Society, 1984] *Giddens Anthony* The Constitution of Society: Outline of a Theory of Structuration, Cambridge; 1984

[Goncalves, Os Portugueses e as minas do Monomotapa: Manica em 1891, 1950]
J Goncalves; Os Portugueses e as minas do Monomotapa, Historia duma Expedicao a Manica em 1891, in Boletim sa Soc. de Geographia de Lisboa, Series 68, no. 9 e 10, Setembro-Outubro, 1950

[Gray R, Annular Eclipse Maps, 1937] *Gray R* Annular Eclipse Maps in JAH Vol. IX 1968 citing G. Lancaster's "Tentative Chronology of the Ngoni: Genealogy of their Chiefs and Notes" in Journal of royal Anthropological Institute XVII ; 1937

[Hall and Stefoff, Great Zimbabwe, 2006] *Hall Martin and Stefoff Rebecca* Great Zimbabwe, Digging for the Past, Oxford University Press; 2006

[Hamdun and King, Ibn Battuta in Black Africa, 2005] *Ibn Battuta* Ibn Battuta In Black Africa, translated by Said Hamdun and Noel King; 2005

BIBLIOGRAPHY

[Hanford, Pre-Colonial South-East Africa: Sources, 2018] *H Matthew Hanford*; Pre-Colonial South-East Africa: Sources and prospects for Research in Economic and Social History, Journal of Southern African Studies 44. 1 – 22; 2018

[Hanlon J, Mozambique, Who Calls the Shots, 1991] *Joseph Hanlon*; Mozambique, Who Calls the Shots; 1991

[Harari, Sapiens: A Brief History of Humankind, 2011] *Harari Yuval Noah* Sapiens: A Brief History of Humankind, Penguin Random House Vintage; 2011

[Hebert Chitepo, An Account of Manyika Kingship, 1958] *Herbert Chitepo*; An Account of Manyika Kingship in Herbert Chitepo's Soko Risina Musoro; 1958

[Hodza and Fortune, Shona Praise Poetry, 1979] *Hodza Aaron and Fortune George* Shona Praise Poetry, Oxford University Press; 1979

[Holland Tom, Athelstan, 2016] *Tom Holland*; Athelstan 924 - 939; 2016

[House, Archaeology of Mapela Hill, South West Zimbabwe, '16] *House Michelle* The Archaeology of Mapela Hill, South-Western Zimbabwe; 2016

[Huffman, Climate Change Shashe Limpopo, 2009] *TN Huffman*; Climate change during the Iron Age in the Shashe Limpopo Basin southern Africa; University of Wits; Journal of Archaeological Science; 2008

[Huffman, Mapungubwe & Great Zimbabwe: Origin of, 2009] *TN Huffman*; Mapungubwe and Great Zimbabwe: the origins and spread of societal complexity in southern Africa; Journal of Anthropological Archaeology; 2009

[Huffman, Mapungubwe and the Origins of the Zimbabwe Culture, 2000] *Huffman TN*; Mapungubwe and the Origins of the Zimbabwe Culture, South African Archaeological Society Goodwin Series; 2000

[Huffman, The Leopard's Kopje Tradition, 1974] *Huffman TN*; The Leopard's Kopje Tradition, Museum Memoir No 6; Harare; 1974

[Huffman, The Soapstone Birds from Great Zimbabwe, 1985] *Huffman TN* The Soapstone Birds from Great Zimbabwe, African Arts Vol 18, No.3, p.68 – 100; 1985

[Hugh Tracey, Descobridor do Monomotapa 1514 – 1515, 1940] *Tracey Hugh* Descobridor do Monomotapa 1514 – 1515, Portuguese translation and notes by Caetano Montez, p36, Maputo; 1940

[Huntingford GWB, Periplus of the Erythreaan Sea, 1980] *Huntingford GWB* Periplus of the Erythreaan Sea, The Hakluyt Society; 1980

[Ibn Battuta, The Travels of Ibn Battuta, 2003] *Ibn Battuta* The Travels of Ibn Battuta, Picador; 2003

[Isaacs, Travels and Adventures in Eastern Africa, 1936] *N Isaacs* Travels and Adventures in Eastern Africa, Cape Town; reprint 1936

[Junod, The Life of a South African Tribe, Lived in Mabhudu 1885-1895, 1912] *HA Junod*; The Life of a South African Tribe, Lived in Mabhudu 1885-1895, Vol I and II, Swiss Romande Mission, 1912

[Kekana, A History of Black people in South Africa to 1795, 1992] *NS Kekana* ; A History of the Black people of South Africa to 1795: a critical analysis of nineteen century South African histiorography, MA History, Univesiy of Visa Johannesburg, 1992

BIBLIOGRAPHY

[Khumalo, Uphoko, 1995] *RS Khumalo*; Uphoko; 1995

[Kienna, Tears for my Land: A Social History of the Kva, 2010] *Kienna* Tears for my Land: A Social History of the Kva of the Central Kalahari Game Reserve, Tc'amnquoo, Gaborone; 2010

[Lane, Reid, Segobye, Ditswa Mmung: Archaeology of Botswana, '99] *Paul Lane, Andrew Reid and Alinah Segobye* Ditswa Mmung; The Archaeology of Botswana, Pula Press, Gaborone; 1999

[Liesegang G, Dingane's attack on Lourenco Marques, 1969] *Liesegang G*; Dingane's attack on Lourenco Marques in 1833; Journal of African History X, 1969

[Liesegang, Internal Gaza Kingdom, Mozambique 1840 – 1895, 1981] *G Liesegang*; Notes on the Internal Structure of the Gaza kingdom of Southern Mozambique 1840 – 1895, in Before and After Nguni History, ed JB Peires, Makhanda Grahamstown SA; 1981

[Liesegang, Nguni Migrations between Delagoa Bay & Zambezi 1821-1839, 1970] *G Liesegang* Nguni Migrations between Delagoa Bay and the Zambezi 1821 -1839, African Historical Studies, vol. 3, no.2, pp. 317-337; 1970

[Lobato A, Expansao Portuguesa em Mocambique de 1498 a 1530, 1935] *Lobato A*; A Expansao Portuguesa em Mocambique de 1498 a 1530, Vol. II; 1935

[Machiridza, Landscapes & Ethnicity: Hist. Archaeology of Khami, 2020] *Machiridza Lesley Hatipone* Landscapes and Ethnicity: An Historical Archaeology of Khami-Phase Site in Southwestern Zimbabwe, Springer; 2020

[Magema ka Fuze, The Black People and whence they came: A Zulu View, 1979] *Magema ka Fuze*; The Black People and whence they came: A Zulu View, translated by HC Lugg; Durban; 1979

[Malaba, The Mwali of Njelele and the Story of BaKalanga, 2011] *Malaba Tshidzanani* The Mwali of Njelele and the Story of BaKalanga; 2011

[Matenga, The Soapstone Birds of Great Zimbabwe, 1998] *Matenga Edward* The Soapstone Birds of Great Zimbabwe: Symbols of a Nation, African Publishing Group; 1998

[Mathebula and Mokgoatsana, Reconstructing Changamire's Family Roots.., 2018] *Mandla Mathebula and Sekgothe Mokgoatsana*; Reconstructing Changamire's Family Roots: New Evidence from the Valoyi Oral History, University of Limpopo; 2018

[Mathebula et al., Tsonga History Perspectives, 2006] *Mathebula, Nkuna, Mabasa, Maluleke* ; Tsonga History Perspectives; 2006

[Mathebula, 800 Years of Tsonga History, 2002] *M Mathebula* ; 800 Years of Tsonga History, Polokwane; 2002

[Mathebula, Genealogy and Migration of Valoyi of Limpopo, 2018] *Mathebula*; Genealogy and Migration of the Va Ka Valoyi People of Limpopo Province South Africa, PhD, University of Limpopo; 2018

[Matsebula, Izakhiwo Zama Swazi, 1953] *JSM Matsebula*; Izakhiwo Zama Swazi; Johannesburg; 1953

[Mda Zakes, The Sculptors of Mapungubwe, 2013] *Zakes Mda* The Sculptors of Mapungubwe, Seagull Books; 2013

BIBLIOGRAPHY

[Mogodi Sol Plaatje, Mahikeng Diary, 1973] *Solomon Mogodi* also known as Sol. T. Plaatje; A Diary of the Siege of Mahikeng; 1973

[Mogodi Sol Plaatje, Mhudi, 1930] *Solomon Mogodi* also known as Sol. T. Plaatje; Mhudi; 1930

[Mogodi Sol Platje, Native Life In South Africa, 1914] *Solomon Mogodi* also known as Sol. T. Plaatje; Native Life in South Africa, 1914

[Molema, The Bantu, Past and Present; Edimburgo, 1920] *SM Molema*; The Bantu, Past and Present; Edimburgo, 1920

[Morais, Early Farming Communties of Southern Mozambique , '88] *JM Morais* The early Farming Communities of Southern Mozambique, Eduardo Mondlane University Mozambique, Central Board of National Antiquities Sweden, Studies in African Archaeology; 1988

[Mtetwa, A history of Uteve under Mwenemutapa rulers 1480 – 1834, 1984] *AH Mtetwa*; A history of Uteve under Mwenemutapa rulers 1480 – 1834: A Re-evaluation; 1984

[Mudenge, A Political History of Munhumutapa c1400 – 1902, 1988] *Mudenge SIG*; A Political History of Munhumutapa, Harare; 1988

[Mudenge, The Rozwi Empire and the Feira in Zumbo, 1972] *Mudenge SIG*; The Rozwi Empire and the Feira in Zumbo, Thesis, pp 35-43, London; 1972

[Mukwende, The Archaeology of Khami and the Butua State, 2020] *Mukwende Tawanda* The Archaeology of Khami and the Butua State, Oxford Research Encyclopaedia, African History; 2020

[Munjeri, The Reunification of the Stone Bird of Great Zimbabwe, 2003] *Munjeri Dawson* The Reunification of the Stone Bird of Great Zimbabwe at an Exhibition of the Tervuren Royal Museum for Central Africa, Belgium ans its return from Germany to Zimbabwe; 14 May 2003

[Mwale, The Ngoni of Nyasaland, 1956] *Mwale* Account by Ishmael Mwale in Margaret Read, The Ngoni of Nyasaland, London; 1956

[Naidu, Three Tales of Theal: Biography, History and Ethnography, 2012] *Naidu Sam* Three Tales of Theal: Biography, History and Ethnography on the Eastern Frontier, English in Africa 39 No. 2, p.51 – 68; 1989

[Ndlovu BD, Laphuma Elinye Lingakatshoni, 2011] *BD Ndlovu*; Laphuma Elinye Lingakatshoni; 2011

[Ndlovu SJ, Icala Lezinduna, 2011] *SJ Ndlovu*; Icala Lezinduna; 2011

[Ndoro, Great Zimbabwe, 2005] *W Ndoro* Great Zimbabwe, Scientific American, University of Cape Town; 2005

[NdzimuUnami Moyo, The Rebirth of BuKalanga, 2012] *Ndzimu Unami E. Moyo*; The Rebirth of Bukalanga, A Manifesto for the Liberation of a Great People; 2012

[Newitt, A History of Mozambique, 1995] *Newitt M*; A History of Mozambique, Hurst and Company, London; 1995

[Newitt, The Zambezi Prazos, 1967] *Newitt M*; The Zambezi Prazos..., PhD, London; 1967

[Obioma Chigozie, The Firshermen, 2015] *Obioma Chigozie*; The Firshermen; Pushkin Press; 2015

BIBLIOGRAPHY

[Omer-Cooper, The Zulu aftermath: 19th century revolution in Bantu Africa, 1966] ***Omer-Cooper***; The Zulu aftermath: the nineteenth century revolution in Bantu Africa; 1966

[Opland J, The First Novel in Xhosa, 2007] ***Jeff Opland***; The First Novel in Xhosa; 2007

[Ostrom, The Evolution of Institutions for Collective Action, 2011] ***Elinor Olstrom***; Governing the Commons; The Evolution of Institutions for Collective Action; 2011

[Pacheco, Viagem de Tete ao Zumbo; Boletim de Mocambique, 1883] ***AM Pacheco***; Viagem de Tete ao Zumbo; Boletim Official do Governo Geral da Provincia de Mocambique, Maputo, Imprensa Nacional 1883

[Pathisa Nyathi, Zimbabwe's Cultural Heritage, 2005] ***Pathisa Nyathi*** Zimbabwe's Cultural Heritage, AmaBooks Publishers; 2005

[Peires JB, The House of Phalo, 1981] ***JB Peires***; The House of Phalo; A History of the Xhosa People in the Days of their Independence; 1981

[Perreira et al., A Prehistoric & Historic traces of mtDNA of Mozambique, 2001] ***Perreira, Macaulay, Torroni, Scozzari, Prata, Amorim***; A Prehistoric and Historic traces of mtDNA of Mozambique: Insights into the Bantu expansions and the slave trade, Ann.Hum.Genet; 2001

[Pikirayi, Ceramics, Global Networks of Trade and Interaction, 2012] ***Pikirayi Innocent*** Ceramics, Global Networks of Trade and Interaction – the feira trade and the Portuguese in northern Zimbabwe 16th – 17th centuries AD, University of Pretoria; 2012

[Pikirayi, Great Zimbabwe in Historical Archaeology, 2013] ***Pikirayi Innocent*** Great Zimbabwe in Historical Archaeology: Reconceptualizing Decline, Abandonment and Reoccupation of an Ancient Polity AD 1450 – 1900; 2013

[Posselt FWT, Fact & Fiction: A short account of Southern Rhod., 1935] ***Posselt FWT*** Fact and Fiction: A short account of the natives of Southern Rhodesia, Bulawayo; 1935

[Randles, L'empire du Monomotapa du XV au XIX siecle, 1975] ***WGL Randles*** L'empire du Monomotapa du XV au XIX siecle, Paris; 1975

[Ransford O, The Rulers of Rhodesia, 1968] ***O Ransford***; *The Rulers of Rhodesia*; 1968

[Read, Interviews with Ishmael Mwale by M. Read, 1935 – 1939] ***Margaret Read*** Interviews Conducted with Ishmael Mwale 1835 – 1839 the treasurer to Inkhosi Gomani II, The Ngoni of Nyasaland, London; 1956

[Rita-Ferreira, Fixacao Port. e Historia Pre-Colonial de Mocambique, '82] ***Rita-Ferreira A*** Fixacao Portuguesa e Historia Pre-Colonial de Mocambique, Instituto de Investigacao Cientifica Tropical com Junta de Investigacaoes Cientificas do Ultramar, No. 142, Lisboa; 1982

[Robert Moffat, The Matebele Journals of Robert Moffat 1829 – 1860, 1860] ***Robert Moffat*** The Matebele Journals of Robert Moffat 1829 – 1860, Vol. II; 1725

[Robinson CH, History of Christian Missions, 1915] ***CH Robinson***; History of Christian Missions; International Theological Library; 1915

[Robinson, Empire of Monomotapa, 1958] ***Robinson***; *Empire of Monomotapa*; 1958

BIBLIOGRAPHY

[Samkange, Origins of Rhodesia, 1968] **Samkange**; Origins of Rhodesia, London; 1968

[Santos JD, Ethiopia Oriental e Historia do Oriente, c.1622] **Joao dos Santos** Ethiopia Oriental e varia historia de cousas notaveis do Oriente; c.1622

[Schoff WH, Periplus of the Erythreaan Sea, 1912] **Schoff WH** Periplus of the Erythreaan Sea, New York; 1912

[Sibanda MM, uMbiko kaMadlenya, 2011] **Mayford M. Sibanda**; uMbiko ka-Madlenya; 2011

[Sinclair PJJ et al., Analyses of slag, iron and ceramics..., 1988] **PJJ Sinclair et al.** Analyses of slag, iron, ceramics and animal bones from excavations in Mozambique, Studies in African Archaeology 2, Eduardo Mondlane University Mozambique, Central Board of National Antiquities Sweden; 1988

[Teju Cole, Known and Strange Things, 2016] **Teju Cole**, Known and Strange Things, Essays by Teju Cole 2016

[Teju Cole, Open City, 2011] **Teju Cole**, Open City ; 2011

[The Periplus of the Erythreaan Sea, 1980] **Periplus of the Erythreaan Sea** by Anonymous in AD 40 – 70, Periplus of the Erythreaan Sea, The Hakluyt Society, London; 1980

[Thompson, Moshoeshoe of Lesotho, 1975] **L Thompson** Surviving in Two Worlds: Moshoeshoe of Lesotho 1786-1870, Oxford Clarendon Press; 1975

[Tlou and Campbell, History of Botswana, 1984] **Tlou Thomas and Campbell Alec** History of Botswana, Macmillan; 1984

[Torres, Estudo da penetracao portuguesa na Africa Oriental, seculo XVI, 1938] **J Torres**; Esboco de estudo da penetracao portuguesa na Africa oriental no seculo XVI, in I Congresso da Historia da Expancao Portuguesa no Mundo, 4a seccao; Lisboa, 1938

[Unknown, Journal of First Voyage of Vasco da Gama 1497-1499, 1898] **Unknown Author translated by EG Ravenstein** A Journal of the First Voyage of Vasco da Gama 1497-1499, The Gutenberg project, The Hakluyt Society; 1898

[Vaal, De Roi Van Joao Albasini in Die Geskiendenis van Transvaal, ????] **JB Vaal**; De Roi Van Joao Albasini in Die Geskiendenis van Transvaal; YYYY???

[Van Waarden, Mosothwane, Leopard's Kopje Burial, 2013] **C Van Waarden and MN Mosothwane**; A Leopard's Kopje Burial at Mathangwane in Northeaster Botswana; University of Botswana; 2013

[Van Waarden, The Origin of Zimbabwe Tradition Walling, 2011] **Van Waarden Catrien** The Origin of Zimbabwe Tradition Walling; Zimbabwe Prehistory 29:54–77; 2011

[Vico Giambattista, A New Science, 1725] **Vico Giambattista** A New Science; 1725

[Vilakazi FM, Ukuduka kwesizwe Zidukelane Nesizwe Zakubo, 1948] **FM Vilakazi**; Ukuduka Kwesizwe Zidukelane Nesizwe Zakubo; Original Manuscript; 1948

[Vusamazulu Credo Mutwa, Indaba, My Children, 1964] **Vusamazulu Credo Mutwa** Indaba, My Children:African Tribal History, Legends, Customs and Religious Beliefs; 1964

[Warmelo, A Preliminary Survey of the Bantu Tribes of South Africa, 1935] **NJv Warmelo**; A Preliminary Survey of the Bantu Tribes of South Africa ; 1935

BIBLIOGRAPHY

[Warmelo, History of Matiwane & AmaNgwane as told by Msebenzi to Hlongwane, 1938]
NJv Warmelo; The History of Matiwane and the AmaNgwane Tribe: As Told by Msebenzi to his kinsman Albert Hlongwane; 1938 [NJv Warmelo, The History of Matiwane and AmaNgwane, 1938]

[Webb and Wright, Stuart archive of recorded oral evidence of AmaZulu history, 1984]
C Webb and JB Wright; The James Stuart Archive of recorded oral evidence to the history of the Zulu and the neighbouring peoples Vol 1 – 4; University of Natal, Durban; 1978 – 1984

[Welch, South Africa under King Manuel, 1943] *SR Welch*; South Africa under King Manuel; Cape Town, 1943

[Wilmot Alexander, Monomotapa its Monuments and its History, 1896] *Alexander Wilmot*; Monomotapa its Monuments and its History from the Most Ancient Times to the Present; Londres, 1896

[Wood et al., Zanzibar & Indian Ocean Trade 1000 CE: Glass Beads, '17] *Wood, Panighello, Orgesa et al.* Zanzibar and Indian Ocean Trade in the First Millennium CE: The Glass Beads Evidence, Archaeology and Anthropological Sciences, Springer Link; 2017

[Wood M., Glass Beads & Pre-European Trade Shashe-Limpopo, 2005] *Wood Marilee* Glass Beads and Pre-European Trade in the Shashe-Limpopo Region, WITS PhD; 2005

First hand accounts in Portuguese

[Documentos Sobre os Portugueses em Mocambique/Africa 1497-1840]
Documents on the Portuguese in Mozambique and Central Africa 1497 – 1840; Documentos Sobre os Portugueses em Mocambique e na Africa Austral 1497 – 1840; Edited under the auspices of the and National Archives of Rhodesia and Nyasaland and Centro de Estudos Historicos Ultramarinos, Lisbon, Volumes 1–6 covering for the period 1497 – 1588; 1962

Vol.I	1497 – 1506 1962
Vol.II	1507 – 1510 1963
Vol.III	1511 – 1514 1964
Vol.IV	1515 – 1516 1965
Vol.V	1617 – 1518 1966
Vol.VI	1519 – 1537 1969
Vol.VII	1540 – 1560 1971
Vol.VIII	1561 – 1588 1975

[Barros, Da Asia: Dos Feitos, Que os Portugueses Fizeram..., 1778] *Joao de Barros*; Da Asia: Dos Feitos, Que os Portugueses Fizeram no Descubrimento, e Conquista dos Mares, e Terras do Oriente, Lisboa; MDCCLXXVII, 1496 – 1570; 1777 Vol.I Decada Primeira, Parte Primeira, MDCCLXXVII 1777 – Vol.II Decada Primeira, Parte Segunda, MDCCLXXVIII 25 de Fevereiro de 1778 – Vol.III Vol.IV Vol.V Vol.VI Vol.VII Vol.VIII Vol.IX

[Couto, Da Asia: Dos Feitos, Que os Portugueses Fizeram..., 1778] *Diogo Couto*; Da Asia: Dos Feitos, Que os Portugueses Fizeram no Descubrimento, e Conquista

BIBLIOGRAPHY

dos Mares, e Terras do Oriente, Lisboa; Anno MDCCLXXVIII 1778 Vol.X Vol.XI Vol.XII

Vol.XXII Decada Duodecima; Parte Ultima Ano MDCCLXXXVIII 1788

[Alcacova, Carta de Diogo de Alcacova para el-Rei CC, 1506] *D Alcacova*; Carta de Diogo de Alcacova para el-Rei; Corpo Cronologico (CC), in Documentos sobre os Portugueses em Mocambique e na Africa Central 1497-1840, Lisbon, Centro de Estudos Historicos Ultramarinos, 1962-3 (1506)

[Alcacova, Carta do Monomotapa SD, 1620] *D Alcacova*; Carta do Monomotapa SD 1620; Documentos Remetidos da India ou Livro das Moncoes (DRILM)

[Alcantara, Inquerito de ano 1573, 1960] *Alcantara G*; Inquerito de ano 1573; Studia no. 6, Lisbon 1960

[Almada JV, Letter from JV Almada in Sofala to the King, 1516] *JV Almada*; Letter from JV Almada to the King, Sofala 26 June 1516 TT-CC 1 Feb 1964, Cited in Lobato, A, A Expansao Portuguesa em Mocambique de 1498 – 1530 Livro II, Politica da Capitancia de Sofala e Mocambique de 1508 a 1530, Agencia Geral do Ultramar, Lisbon, 1954, p49; 1516

[Barbossa, Esmeralso Orbis, 1892] *Duarte Barbossa*; Esmeraldo Orbis; 1892

[Barbossa, Esmeralso Orbis, 1892] *D de Mello de Castro*; Noticia do Imperio Marave e dos Rios de Sena; Anais da Junta de Investigacoes do Ultramar 9, 1954

[Bocarro, Decada 13a. da Historia da India, 1876] *Antonio Bocarro*; Decada 13a. da Historia da India; Lisboa; 1876

[Brito, Letter from Francisco de Brito, 1519] *F Brito*; Letter from Francisco de Brito, factor at Sofala, to the King 8/8/1519 in Theal's RSEA Vol. I, p 103 –107, Cape Town; 1964

[Capello and Ivens, Letter from the Viceroy to the King, 1694] *Capello and Ivens*; Letter from the Vicery fo India to the King 16 October 1694 in Capello and Ivens. in "Travaux des Portugais au Monomotapa", Lisbon; 1889

[Correa, Lendas da India, 1858] *Gaspar Correa*; Lendas da India, TOMO I, Lisbon, p573; 1858

[Correa, Lendas da India, 1869] *Gaspar Correa*; Lendas da India, Voyages of Da Gama; 1869

[Cristovao de Tavora, Letter from Cristova, 1518] *Cristovao de Tavora*; Letter from Cristovao de Tavora to the King 1518 – 1519, Carta dos Vice-reis no 143 in Documentos sobre os Portugueses em Mocambique, Vol VI, 1519 – 1537; 1969

[Ferrao AH, Letter from AH Ferrao to the Governor of Quelimane 28/01/1854, 1867] *AH Ferrao*; Letter from Anselmo Henrique Ferrao to the Governor of Quelimane and Rios de Sena 28/01/1854 in "Annaes do Conselho do Ultramarino parte nao official la Serie" p.241, Lisbon; 1867

[Nicolau, Memorias sobre Sofala, 1998] *VH Nicolau*; Memorias sobre Sofala, 1998

[Salt, Voyage to Abyssinia, 1809] *Henry Salt*; Voyage to Abyssinia, 1809 – 1810

[Santos, Ethiopia Oriental e Historia do Oriente, 1609] *Joao Dos Santos*; Ethiopia Oriental e varia historia de couzas notaveis do Oriente; Evora; 1609

[Silveira, Letter to the King, 1517] *Joao da Silveira*; Letter from Joao da Silveira to the King, Mocambique, 14/2/1517; This letter is summarised by A. Lobato in A Expansao Portuguesa em Mocambique de 1498 a 1530, Vol. II; 1935

BIBLIOGRAPHY

[Soares PV, Letter from PV Soares; Documentos Sobre Vol. III, 1513] **PV Soares**; Letter from PV Soares factor at Sofala to the King, 30 June 1513, ANTT CC.1 18-27 in Documentos sobre os Portugueses em Mocambique e na Africa Central 1497 – 1840 Vol. III, p459, National Archives of Rhodesia, Lisbon; 1962

Second hand accounts, ethnography and other studies

[Abraham, The Monomotapa Dynasty NADA, 1959] **DP Abraham**; The Monomotapa Dynasty, NADA, 59 – 86; 1959

[Abraham, Early political history of the kingdom of Mwenemutapa 850-1589, 1962] **DP Abraham**; The early political history of the kingdom of Mwene Mutapa 850 – 1589, in Historians in Tropical Africa, Proceedings of the Leverhulme Intercollegiate History Conference, Bulawayo, 61 – 91; 1962

[Livingstone, Missionary Researches and Travels in South Africa, 1858] **David Livingstone**; Missionary Researches and Travels in South Africa; 1858

[Theal GM, Records of SA Vol 1-6, 1900] **GM Theal**; Records of South Eastern Africa Volume 1 - 6, London, Government of the Cape; 1900

[Theal GM, The Beginning of SA History, 1902] **GM Theal**; The Beginning of South African History, London, 1902

[Theal GM, Africa South of the Zambezi, 1907] **GM Theal**; History and Ethnography of Africa South of the Zambezi, From Settlement of the Portuguese at Sofala in September 1505 to the Conquest of the Cape Colony by the British in September 1795, Volume I of III, London, 1907

Websites

[Afrolegends.com, A Blog about African History, 2013] **Afrolegends**: A Blog about African History and Heritage; 2013

[BBC Pathe Archives, Buried Treasure: King Solomons' Mines, 1958] **BBC Pathe Archives**: Buried Treasure: King Solomon's Mines presented by Sir Mortimer Wheeler; 1958

[Mozambiquedata.wordpress.com, Makombe Dynasty and Sources, 2014] **Mozambiquedata**: Mozambique Data: Makombe Dynasty and Sources; 2014

[Sahistory.org.za, South African History Online, 2013] **SA History**: South African History Online; 2013

[Website.com, Some Website, 1995] **Afrolegends**: Some Website; 1995

www.ingramcontent.com/pod-product-compliance
Lightning Source LLC
Chambersburg PA
CBHW011318080526
44589CB00020B/2744